IT ARCHITECT SERIES:
The Journey

A Guidebook for Anyone
Interested in IT Architecture

Melissa Palmer

 IT ARCHITECT SERIES™

Upper Saddle River, NJ • Boston • Indianapolis • San Francisco New York • Toronto • Montreal • London • Munich • Paris • Madrid Cape Town • Sydney • Tokyo • Singapore • Mexico City

IT Architect Series: The Journey, A Guidebook for Anyone Interested in IT Architecture

Copyright © 2017 Melissa Palmer.

Published by IT Architect Resource, LLC
14 Ansel Street, Salem, New Hampshire 03070
itaseries.com

All rights reserved. No part of this book may be reproduced, stored, or transmitted by any means—whether auditory, graphic, mechanical, or electronic—without written permission of the author, except in the case of brief excerpts used in critical articles and reviews. Unauthorized reproduction of any part of this work is illegal and is punishable by law.

All terms mentioned in this book that are known to be trademarks or service marks have been appropriately capitalized. The publisher cannot attest to the accuracy of this information. Use of a term in this book should not be regarded as affecting the validity of any trademark or service mark.

Cisco, VMware, Veeam, Apache, and VirtualBox terms are trademarks or registered trademarks of Cisco, VMware Veeam, Apache, and VirtualBox in the United States, other countries, or both.

SuperUltraExa, LightSpeedSync, Thirty M Three, DonkeyExpress, and BackFlip Sideways are fictional companies and products, and do not apply to any real company outside of this book. Any resemblance to exiting companies or products is not intentional.

The opinions expressed in this book belong to the author and are not necessarily those of the company they work for.

Warning and Disclaimer

Every effort has been made to make this book as complete and as accurate as possible, but no warranty or fitness is implied. The information provided is on an "as is" basis. The authors and the publisher shall have neither liability nor responsibility to any person or entity with respect to any loss or damages arising from the information contained in this book.

ISBN: 978-1-4834-9656-6 (sc)
ISBN: 978-1-4834-7363-5 (hc)
ISBN: 978-1-4834-9655-9 (e)

Library of Congress Control Number: 2017912542

Because of the dynamic nature of the Internet, any web addresses or links contained in this book may have changed since publication and may no longer be valid. The views expressed in this work are solely those of the author and do not necessarily reflect the views of the publisher, and the publisher hereby disclaims any responsibility for them.

Rev. date: 1/10/2019

DEDICATION

For as long as I can remember, it has always been a dream of mine to write a book. Like most dreams I have had, it has come true thanks to the support of my family. I am where I am today thanks to your endless encouragement. Thank you to my mother, the best teacher, supporter, and friend I could ever ask for. Words are not enough to express the gratitude I have for you.

To my son, the greatest thing I have ever architected. Watching you grow and change every day has been the greatest journey of my life. I love you, and I cannot wait to see what the future brings for you.

My IT architecture journey has been supported by so many along the way. To all of you who have graced me with your most precious resource, your time, I thank you for making me a better IT architect.

Thank you to Mark and John for helping me to begin this particular journey, and for their support during this project.

– Melissa Palmer

CONTENTS

Tables ix
Figures xi
Foreword xiii
Who Should Read This Book xix
Goals and Methods xxi
How to Use This Book.. xxiii
About the Author xxvii
Acknowledgements... xxix
Please Share Your Feedback xxxi
Reader Services xxxiii
About the IT Architect Series xxxv

Part I – Before We Go

Chapter 1:   The Journey Begins... 1
Chapter 2:   What Is an Architect?.. 8
Chapter 3:   Self-Assessment 20
Chapter 4:   Learning New Skills.. 33
Chapter 5:   Academic and Practical IT Architecture 46

Part II – On Our Way

Chapter 6:   Architectural Building Blocks.. 63
Chapter 7:   Infrastructure Areas of Expertise....................................... 80
Chapter 8:   Connecting the Infrastructure Areas of Expertise 107
Chapter 9:   Putting Together the Architectural Building Blocks........136

Part III – You're Almost There

Chapter 10: Certifications and Continued Learning.............................161
Chapter 11: IT Architectural Skills in Practice 173
Chapter 12: The Distance Travelled...184
Chapter 13: The Next Chapter..192

Part IV – Appendices

Appendix A: Self-Assessment Workbook 199
Appendix B: Your First IT Architecture 209
Appendix C: Resources 223
Glossary of Acronyms 231
References..235

TABLES

Table 1 - Skill Assessment Guidelines 23
Table 2 - Sample Technology Skill Self-Assessment............................. 24
Table 3 - Sample Goal for Technology Skill Development.................... 25
Table 4 - Sample Soft Skill Assessment 28
Table 5 - Sample Goal for Soft Skill Development................................ 28
Table 6 - A Listing of 9's.. 66
Table 7 - Thirty M Three, Inc. Tiers of Service 128
Table 8 - Infrastructure Design Quality Ranking 132
Table 9 - Skill Inspiration Ranking 169
Table 10 - Infrastructure Areas of Expertise Inspiration Ranking........169
Table 11 - Architectural Building Block Inspiration Ranking 170

FIGURES

Figure 1 - The Architects 9
Figure 2 - Conceptual Diagram 55
Figure 3 - Logical Diagram 56
Figure 4 - Physical Diagram 57
Figure 5 - Logical Diagram, Server and Compute 84
Figure 6 - Logical Diagram, Virtualization... 85
Figure 7 - Logical Diagram, Virtual Machines 87
Figure 8 - Logical Diagram, Network 89
Figure 9 - Logical Diagram, Storage Array.. 92
Figure 10 - Logical Diagram, Web Application 94
Figure 11 - Logical Diagram, Backup and Recovery 96
Figure 12 - Logical Diagram, Business Continuity and Disaster Recovery 98
Figure 13 - Logical Diagram, Security 100
Figure 14 - Comparison of Infrastructure Areas and Components....... 113
Figure 15 - Virtualization Components 118
Figure 16 - IOPS and Cost/Latency of Drive Types 123
Figure 17 - Network Throughput Diagram 126
Figure 18 - The Continued Learning Process................................... 171
Figure 19 - Technology Opportunities...181

FOREWORD

The IT Architect Series was started with the hope that we, as authors, could help others who were looking to enhance their architecture and design skills. There seemed to be a missing segment of books on this type of topic. As we started working on our first book, we quickly realized how much else was missing in the logical approach in solving problems in IT, whether traditional data center or private/public/hybrid cloud.

As we started to think how else we could empower those looking to improve their own IT careers, the number of topics we started to identify became so large, that we had to bring others on board as authors to add their stories and expertise to the IT Architect Series. This seemed like an unmanageable task in our journey to help the community.

Well, we have had an unbelievable outpouring of budding and proven authors who are willing to help this series of books reach vast numbers of those who have chosen IT as a career, and are looking to better themselves. We have had so much feedback from the community that are reading the books in the series, that we are seeing the results of all our efforts we have put forth so far…filling the need for inspiration, guidance, and examples that were missing in published works people could use to learn, not something specific (as there is plenty of material on specific hardware and software), but on the approaches they could take to solving architectural, design, and implementation challenges in their own lives.

The first book, IT Architect Series: Foundations in the Art of Infrastructure Design, was a runaway success. Our second book, IT Architect Series: Designing Risk in IT Infrastructure is already getting amazing feedback from the community. As we were discussing the topics that seem to benefit the community at large, we kept coming back to a topic that most of you reading this book have either asked or have been asked about; "…how do I get started?"

We are excited to see this book, IT Architect Series: The Journey, come to life.

For the veterans of the IT community, this is a great retrospective of things that we have done in our careers. For those getting started or in progress of moving along your chosen career path, this book can provide guidance, ideas, and more importantly...some exercises for you to undertake and map out your path of continuing education and certification (if you like to collect acronyms to add to your email signature).

When we approached Melissa to write this book, she was in the middle of one of the more challenging certifications out there...the VMware Certified Design eXpert (or VCDX). In our minds, this made here the perfect candidate to ask if she could author a book that provided not only her perspective, but provide guidance and assistance for those on a journey in their careers.

The Journey is not always an easy one. Working full time (only 50-80 hours a week), either sponsored (company paid) or self-funded, and dealing with training, study, and lab equipment. Late nights. Not alienating our families and friends. Late nights. Sitting at testing centers getting certified in this vendor or that. Late nights. The mental anguish of failing an exam. Late nights. The joy in passing an exam (yes, even the easy ones!). Did I mention late nights?

We have all done it. Sometimes we even had help along the way. For those of you picking up this book for the first time, give it a good read. Then read it again. You will know you are not alone in seeking out what will help make you happy, while building your knowledge. You will find a mentor along the way (this is important, and easy to do in this age). You will grow personally and professionally ... and then it will be your turn to help someone else start THEIR journey. When you get to that point where someone asks YOU for help, you will find a no more rewarding thing than saying "...yes, of course I will help you..." You will know you are on your way. Will it happen tomorrow? ... No. Nothing good ever comes easy, but that day will come.

In the meantime. The help you are getting from books, co-workers, managers, and the IT community in general should help keep you moving along YOUR journey. Don't let anyone tell you that it is impossible, or too hard to do. We have all done it, and now it's your turn!

Good luck on The Journey you are about to embark on!

John Yani Arrasjid, VCDX-001
DELL EMC Office of the CTO
IT Architect Resource, Managing Partner
Mark Gabryjelski, VCDX-023
Worldcom Exchange Inc., Virtualization Practice Manager
IT Architect Resource, Managing Partner

FOREWORD

Let me start by saying I am old. I started in the technology field in the 1980s at Bell Communications Research. I then worked at financial institutions in a variety of IT roles. I then made a leap to the vendor side working for the major players in the data storage industry. Over the years, I mentored folks at every company I was with.

I mentored Melissa when she joined the vendor side from the customer side of the house. I saw these traits in Melissa:

- The eagerness and ability to learn and grow
- Energy
- Personality - Customers like her!

Melissa has expanded her skill set over the years and I am very proud of her. She became a VMware Certified Design Expert (VCDX) by dedicating her personal time to grow. She has a full-time job, she has a family, yet she spent the time to write this book. This is a great example of how she, like myself, seeks to give back to the technology community.

Each IT architect's journey is unique. Melissa's perspective will be helpful to many aspiring IT architects, and give other readers a glimpse into many areas they may not usually be privy to. The customer experience of being a VMware administrator at a major pharmaceutical company dealing with real world business challenges. She knows how it is in the real world so to speak. She also has a perspective from the vendor side of the house. In her current role, she has learned how technology companies operate and the struggles of meeting the dates on product enhancement and direction. Her experiences as a Sales Engineer gives her a view of the difficulties of bringing in new technology to a new or existing customer.

Melissa has an upbeat personality and enjoys interacting with customers and co-workers. This is a quality that is extremely important for any aspiring IT architect. I have met many brilliant people in my career that did not want to share their knowledge. These folks do not tend to last too long in this industry. Technology is ever changing and we can all learn from each other.

I think the readers of this book are very fortunate to get Melissa's perspective on her journey to becoming an IT architect.

Lou DiBenedetto
Technology Industry Expert and Mentor

WHO SHOULD READ THIS BOOK

This book is for anyone with an interest in IT architecture, regardless of their current experience level.

For aspiring IT architects, this book can be the guide along the journey. It is the book I (and I am sure many others) wish existed when I began my journey to becoming an IT architect.

This book is also a great resource for those who are not sure if they want to be an IT architect. It will give those readers an understanding of what an IT architect does, and what the journey to becoming an IT architect looks like. Likewise, this book is also a resource for those who are interested in finding out more about what IT architects do, no matter where they sit in an organization. Whether you have the role of a project manager, a product manager, a consumer of technology services, or any anything else, if you touch an IT infrastructure, this book is for you.

This book is also a great refresher for experienced IT architects. Whether they are looking to continue their journey with a certification such as the VCDX certification, a job change, or learning new technologies, this book is written for them too.

GOALS AND METHODS

The goal of this book is more than just providing information for the journey to becoming an IT architect.

The lessons I have learned during my own personal IT architecture journey have continued to serve me in all aspects of life. These lessons can apply to anyone, no matter their background or what journey they are starting. Whether you are an aspiring IT architect, or an experienced IT architect, you will find the lessons in this book useful. Whether you are an application owner, a marketing professional, or a CTO you will find these lessons useful.

Beyond developing the skills needed to be an IT architect, this book also focuses on some of the following lessons:

The Power of Self-Reflection
Discovering New Methods of Learning
Strategies for Gaining Different Types of Knowledge
Embracing Change

This is not an exhaustive list of everything you will learn in this book. Many more lessons await you in these pages.

HOW TO USE THIS BOOK

This book is written in the order which I believe will serve you best during journey to becoming an IT architect. This book is meant to be your companion throughout the journey. Feel free to write in it, fold over corners of pages, and add sticky notes to parts you find interesting.

I recommend reading this book through once before you begin to assess your skills and set goals for yourself. If you have already begun your journey, I would also recommend a read through before you start analyzing how far you have come, and what your next steps are to continue your journey.

This book is divided into three distinct parts, and three appendices, which cover the following material:

Part I – Before We Go

Part I is about getting ready to begin your journey to becoming an IT architect. In the first part of this book, you will get into the right mindset, and begin to gather the tools you need to begin your journey in earnest.

Chapter 1, "The Journey Begins" This chapter sets the stage for this book, and introduces the author's journey.

Chapter 2, "What Is an Architect?" This chapter discusses what an IT architect does, and the traits of an IT architect.

Chapter 3, "Self-Assessment" This chapter guides you through the assessment of your own IT architecture skills as you begin your journey.

Chapter 4, "Learning New Skills" This chapter discusses various methods of learning new material and skills.

Chapter 5, "Academic and Practical IT Architecture" This chapter focuses on the difference between academic and practical IT architecture, and what it means to you.

Part II – On Our Way

Part II dives deeper into the core skills required to become an IT architect, and why they are important. Then, we focus on gaining different types of experience with these core skills.

Chapter 6, "Architectural Building Blocks" This chapter introduces the core non-technical skills of an IT architect, why they are important, and what could go wrong if they are ignored.

Chapter 7, "Infrastructure Areas of Expertise" This chapter introduces the core IT infrastructure skills of an IT architect, why they are important, and what could go wrong if they are ignored. It also discusses some newer technologies IT architects are currently working with.

Chapter 8, "Connecting the Infrastructure Areas of Expertise" This chapter examines ways to gain different types of skills in the core IT infrastructure areas an IT architect interacts with.

Chapter 9, "Putting Together the Architectural Building Blocks" This chapter details how to gain the non-technical skills required of an IT architect.

Part III – You're Almost There

Part III discusses more areas an IT architect is concerned with, as they continue their journey.

Chapter 10, "Certifications and Continued Learning" This chapter talks about the IT industry certifications, and continuing to learn about the areas visited during the journey.

Chapter 11, "IT Architectural Skills in Practice" This chapter discusses how IT architects can begin to use their skillset during their day to day activities, including changing jobs.

Chapter 12, "The Distance Travelled" This chapter focuses on self-reflection, and lessons learned during the journey.

Chapter 13, "The Next Chapter" The next chapter of your IT architecture journey begins here, where you will learn one of the most important secrets of the IT architect.

Part IV – Appendices

Part IV contains appendices to help you along your IT architecture journey.

Appendix A, "Self-Assessment" A guided self-assessment to help you determine where you are in your IT architecture journey.

Appendix B, "Your First Architecture" A fictional customer's scenario, along with a guide to creating your first IT architecture design.

Appendix C, "Resources" Ideas for gaining knowledge on your journey, together in one easy to read appendix.

ABOUT THE AUTHOR

Melissa Palmer, VCDX-236, is an information technology infrastructure enthusiast. She has held various roles such as Technical Marketing Engineer, Solutions Architect, Systems Engineer, and Infrastructure Analyst during her career.

Melissa has always had a passion for learning. She began taking technology courses at community college at the age of 14. She dropped out of high school after three years to attend college at Stevens Institute of Technology in Hoboken, New Jersey. At Stevens, Melissa earned a Bachelor of Engineering degree in Electrical Engineering. She went on to earn a Master of Engineering Degree in Networked Information Systems focused on Secure Networked Systems Design.

During her time at Stevens, she was an infrastructure intern for an online bond trading firm on Wall Street. She began her career in the IT infrastructure organization of a pharmaceutical company working with a number of infrastructure technologies. She began working with Virtualization in 2007, which began her journey to becoming an IT architect. In 2012, she made the transition from customer to vendor.

Melissa is active in the IT infrastructure community. She is also the Creative Director of the Virtual Design Master program (**http://virtualdesignmaster.io**), which provides technology community members the opportunity to work on their IT architecture skills with the mentorship of IT architects. When Melissa is not working with technology, she enjoys going to rocket launches, cooking, and writing. More of her writing can be found on her own blog located at **http://vMiss.net/**. Follow her on Twitter **@vMiss33**.

ACKNOWLEDGEMENTS

The author would like to thank the following people for their support in developing and reviewing the material included in this book.

After completing your IT architecture journey, you will be empowered to continue it in a number ways. For the author, it was beginning the long-awaited journey of writing this book. For others, it was becoming part of the *IT Architect Series* by dedicating their time to review the content of this book and the other books in the series.

Thank you to the following for contributing to this book through their guidance on the IT architecture journey. Thank you to Eric Wright and Angelo Luciani, for bringing me on to the Virtual Design Master Creative Team, and jump starting my journey in earnest. Thank you to Lou DiBenedetto for your guidance and friendship, you taught me the way things should be done. Thank you to Ron Wedel, Jason Grierson, Shady Ali ElMalatawey, Rene van den Bedem, Gregg Robertson, Josh Odgers, and Michael Webster for your mentorship along the journey. Forming a study group is a big part of the journey, thank you to the VCDX Wolfpack for being my sounding board and support system. Thank you to Sean Sabaski for the countless hours you spent showing me what this VMware thing was all about. Thank you to Zeen Rachidi for the cover art.

Thank you to reviewers including the above individuals for your time and effort. John Arrasjid, Doug Baer, Daemon Behr, Gareth Edwards, Mark Gabryjelski, Farah Kahn, Angelo Luciani, Manish Patel, and Paul Woodward Jr.

Melissa Palmer, VCDX-236

PLEASE SHARE YOUR FEEDBACK

As authors and IT architects, we recognize and value your feedback on what we are doing well, areas to improve, and new content you feel would benefit those perusing a role as an infrastructure design architect. If there are other topic areas you believe would be valuable to the IT Architect Series, we are here to listen. We are working with additional authors to continue the series with material tied to various areas of infrastructure design.

When you share your feedback, please be sure to include this book's title, along with your name, e-mail address, and phone number. We will carefully review your comments but may not be able to provide a direct response to all submissions. Thank you for sharing with us.

Mail: IT Architect Resource, LLC, Salem, NH 03079
Website: www.itaseries.com

READER SERVICES

Visit the book website

http://www.itaseries.com
or
http://www.itarchitectseries.com

Register this book for convenient access to any updates, downloads, or errata that might be available for this book.

ABOUT THE IT ARCHITECT SERIES

The world of infrastructure continues to evolve. As it does, there are both aspiring and experienced individuals developing, deploying, and supporting traditional and new types of infrastructures. We have evolving virtual and cloud solutions that continue to mature, while introducing new challenges and new players in this area.

Infrastructure design involves much more than technology. Just because something is built and running does not mean it is easy to use, or is adaptable to evolving business needs. IT Architects must deal with multiple vendors, technologies, skills, people, and process in a way to seamlessly support the needs of a business.

John Yani Arrasjid (VCDX-001) and Mark Gabryjelski (VCDX-23) took the journey and achieved one of the most recognized certifications in this space. They talked to publishers but could not find one that recognized the value of a series of books for IT Architects, so they created their own. In addition, they provided a more author friendly environment that provided greater benefits to the authors.

The first book in the series, *Foundation in the Art of Infrastructure Design*, was the start of this series, formed under IT Architect Resource, LLC. The goal was to provide a missing source of information and reference for both established architects, and those looking to become an architect.

Most of the books in the series include the three stages of design. Conceptual models are developed during the initial gathering of input, and with design discussions to develop the customer's perspective and vision. Logical designs lay out technical and operational capabilities and a framework to select products and configurations. The physical model and design lay out the details of the technology, configurations, and operations. These three stages allow for interactive dialogue with the business teams to reach consensus on a solution supporting the needs of today and the future.

The latest books in the series, including the one you are reading now, provide details in specific domains that we believe provide additional value. In each book we include stories, examples, recommendations, and exercises. The series of books support the training and are a reference source on your journey of as an IT architect.

We encourage feedback on what you would like to see added to the series. For a full list of series books, to share your feedback, and to join the growing list of authors, please see www.itaseries.com. We look forward to hearing from you!

PART I
BEFORE WE GO

CHAPTER 1

THE JOURNEY BEGINS

"A man who dares to waste one hour of time has not discovered the value of life."
— Charles Darwin

I do not think I can pinpoint the moment when I decided to begin the journey of becoming an Information Technology (IT) architect. I have always found the world of IT architecture fascinating, and almost naturally gravitated in that direction during my career. I can, however, tell you the moment when the lightbulb went off in my head on how I could prove it. It was the year 2010. I had been browsing the VMware Certification website, and came across something called the VMware Certified Design Expert (VCDX) certification.

It was not so much the letters that called to me, but the description of what a successful candidate should be able to do. Six years later, I became VCDX-236, but it was not the magical number that made me an IT architect.

The Beginning of My Journey

I need to start long before that fateful day in 2010, if I want to talk about how I became an IT architect. When I thought long and hard about my journey after I had achieved the VCDX certification, I realized it started long before my career ever did. I was exposed to technology as a child, and immediately became interested in it. Growing up there were other things that interested me as well. I wanted to be a doctor or a pharmacist at times, but at the end of the day, it all kept coming back to technology.

Chances are if you think back on what led you to pick up your book, your journey began long before your career in IT did. There had to be a reason you became interested in this field at some point. Of all the careers you could have picked, there was something which made you decide on this one. Whatever that something is, and whatever path you took to get here, I am glad you have made it this far.

When I really started thinking about it, it was easy for me to see when my journey began. My father is a network architect, and I was exposed to technology (and more importantly, networking) starting around the time I was eight years old. He taught me things like binary and programming at home, and I started taking networking classes at a community college when I was 14 years old. I completely fried the first computer I ever tried to build from spare parts, but we do not talk about that any more.

I really, really liked networking, and figured it was my thing for sure. As we all know, you do not really go to college for networking alone. When I was 16, I dropped out of high school to go and study Electrical Engineering at Stevens Institute of Technology (coincidentally, this is what my dad had studied too). This was a big decision point for me. Originally, when I started looking at universities, I wanted to study Computer Science. However, I could not find an academic program that I thought was really interesting. There was too much other stuff in there I did not really want to bother with. This made me begin to look at Engineering programs, which were quite a bit different.

One great thing about a Bachelor's of Engineering degree (which Stevens is one of the few places in the United States to offer) is the time spent by students all areas of engineering, and the actual design work done in these various areas. The things I learned at Stevens carried across to the real world once I graduated, except for calculus. I hate calculus.

I was also lucky enough to spend time as an infrastructure intern at an electronic bond trading firm on Wall Street during my time at Stevens. For me, this confirmed how much I loved IT infrastructure, especially networking.

I did not realize as a senior in college, that my trajectory was about to change. I was interviewing with a senior infrastructure director, and he mentioned this little thing called VMware. I had no idea what it was, so I went and searched for it on Google after the interview. I had no idea this encounter was one of the first things which would begin to shape my career.

My Journey to Becoming an IT Architect

For me, becoming an IT architect was something that made sense. I knew this, as when I began my career I was always fascinated by more than just my tiny piece of the puzzle. I also realized it was not going to happen overnight. The people who were kind enough to take the time out of their busy days to explain their piece of the puzzle to me had much, much more experience than I did. I realized, early on, it was going to take a lot of hard work and learning to get me to where I ultimately wanted to be.

Knowing where you want to get to, and knowing how to get there are two completely different things. Getting there requires patience and time, first and foremost. You are not going to become an IT architect overnight, no matter how badly you want to. It is also going to require leaps of faith. One day you are going to realize you are sorely lacking in some sort of experience you need to become an IT architect, and you are going to have to take a leap of faith to get it, which may be completely terrifying.

I did not wake up one morning and realize I was an IT architect. It was something that happened gradually over time. During the course of the journey, you will however notice yourself changing. You will look at work you did a year ago, and wonder how you ever created it because it is just so far below your standards of today (even though it was the best thing you ever did last year). Becoming an architect is as much about the journey to get there as it is the end goal.

The Journey Is What You Make of It

While we know our end goal is to become an IT architect, the journey itself is what enables you to meet this goal. Over and over you will hear people say things like "It is about the journey." and "The journey is what you make of it.". I did not truly understand these sayings until I began my own journey. The journey may be full of stops and starts. It may take longer than you originally planned it to take. Some parts of the journey may be harder than others. The journey will be full of lessons to be learned.

The journey is truly what you make of it. You are in control of your journey, so it is up to you how you the lessons are learned. It is up to you to decide which skills you need to gain along the way. It is up to you to decide what pace you take. The journey is yours and yours alone, so be sure to mold it however you want. There is no right or wrong path to take on the journey, since it is different for everyone.

Be sure to enjoy it. Relish in the experiences you are gaining. It is ok to take it slow at some points because you are enjoying it so much. It is ok to speed it up when you need to because of personal or professional commitments. Make sure you seek out others on who are also on the journey. One of the best parts of this journey will be the people you meet. You will meet them when you least expect it, and you will forge friendships. While the journey is yours, you may meet people you can collaborate with, and you may even be able to travel parts of the path together. Be sure to keep this in the back of your mind during the journey.

Reflection at the Highest Peak

The highest peak I have reached so far on my journey is achieving the VCDX certification. After receiving the e-mail with my VCDX number, I began to reflect on my journey, and on myself as an IT architect. If I looked at the content I began developing as I started VCDX design, and the final product, it was completely different. In just the course of writing my design, and associated documentation, I had grown tremendously as an IT architect.

In 2006, I did not even know what VMware was. When I look back on this simple fact today, I can barely fathom it. Today, I know more about VMware technologies than I ever could have imagined so many years ago. In 2007, when I ended up working on a team under that same senior director who interviewed me, I started using these technologies. I went from designing a two VMware ESX host environment as my first ever vSphere design to successfully defending a much larger VMware design as part of gaining my VCDX certification in 2016. I was working with VDI before it was even called VDI, when the technology was just getting started.

Today, I would architect a two node ESXi environment much differently than I did back then. When I was first getting started with virtualization, I was still trying to figure out how everything worked, and what parts needed to go together. It was a constant stop and start, as I realized I had reached another dependency and required something else from another team, like a network switch configuration or storage for my VMware ESX hosts. At the end of the day I had a working cluster of ESX hosts, but the path I had taken to get there was winding and full of rough terrain.

During the journey, we will grow not only as IT architects, but as people. Learning and growing does not discount anything we did beforehand. It does not automatically make everything we did before worthless. The things you have accomplished up to now have shaped you into the technologist you are today. Could I have architected that very first VMware ESX environment differently? Of course I could have, but that does not mean I did not end up with a solution which met my requirements at the end of the day (I can tell you now, I was not even thinking of things in terms of requirements back then).

I have another funny story I like to tell about my early days working with VMware. This took place during VMworld, which is the annual VMware conference, in 2008. No, sadly, I did not get to go, but the senior gentleman on my team was nice enough to offer me his swag. Anyway, he did go, which means he handed the keys of the kingdom over to me before he left.

My Monday morning started with an ESX host biting the dust, and failing. It was a VMware ESX 2.5.4 host, so the environment did not have any of these fancy clusters or features to restart the VMs after a failure. I also did not have the password to this host, since I was working primarily with the shiny new VMware ESX 3.5 environment. After I finally tracked down someone to connect to the console of the server, it turned out the server just needed a reboot. After explaining to them how to reboot it (type reboot, hit enter, it was not exactly rocket science), I breathed a huge sigh of relief.

Until, later that same day, one of the ESX 3.5 hosts failed. No big deal, right? The VMware High Availability feature restarted my virtual machines on surviving hosts, just like it was supposed to. However, this just reminded us we really needed the host's capacity. This was 2008, and it was all about virtualizing everything in sight. The next couple of days were spent finishing up the paper work to bring another brand new ESX 3.5 cluster online.

Back then, my mind was blown by the fact I could operate this environment, when I had just started working with the technology the year before. Even when I think back to it now, I am still proud of how far I had come in such a short time. Now years later, as a VCDX, the work I did at the beginning of my career is still relevant. It helped to shape me into the IT architect I am today.

What This Book Is For

It is hard to put into words just how much I learned during the journey. When it came to learning these new things, I found methods and resources which worked quite well for me, and other things just crashed and burned no matter how hard I tried to make them work. My goal is to teach you the things that did in fact work well. By using this book, you have the benefit of what I wish I would have known when I started my journey to becoming an IT architect.

I want this book to be your guide along the journey. I want you to put sticky notes all over it, write on the pages in it (especially the Self-Assessment Workbook in Appendix A!), and wear it out. I want this book to be the guide I did not have when I started out. When I present you with ideas on how to gain the skills you will need to become an IT architect, I am using the knowledge I gained during my journey to guide you. I will also share the lessons I learned on my journey with you.

The Journey Starts Here

I can give you recommendations on learning methods and resources. I can give you examples of what worked well for me on my journey, and the tips and tricks I picked up along the way. I can give you endless amounts of information, but I cannot give you everything.

There is one vital thing you are going to need to embark on this journey. This is the drive and determination to become an IT architect. The best piece of advice I have ever gotten in my life is from my mother, which is "ALWAYS GIVE 110%". You are going to need this drive to get you through the rough patches, and to keep you up late at night working.

CHAPTER 2

WHAT IS AN ARCHITECT?

> *"The significant problems we face cannot be solved at the same level of thinking we were at when we created them."*
> — *Albert Einstein*

Architects have been around since the beginning of time. This planet is full of the ruins of the civilizations which came before us, designed by their architects. They built the Seven Wonders of the Ancient World. They built the Great Pyramid of Giza. They built the Hanging Gardens of Babylon. Imagine being the architect of the Great Pyramid of Giza. Imagine, after many years of painstaking planning on endless rolls of papyrus, you begin to see the fruits of your labor. The structure you designed slowly rises to a total height of 481 feet. Would you have imagined your pyramid would remain the tallest structure in the world for over 3,800 years? Over 4,500 years later, people continue to marvel at this architectural wonder.

The Architect

The word architect as we know it today comes from the Greek word **arkhitekton** or chief (**arki**) builder (**tekton**). There are many types of architects, ranging from structural architects to IT architects. When we hear the word **architect**, we tend to think of the former. In this book, we are going to explore the world of the IT architect. You may be wondering who is the IT architect? What role do they play in the economy today? What do they do every day? What is the process to build an IT infrastructure environment from their perspective?

No matter what is being designed and constructed, architecture itself has some common tenets. At their core, architects design with blueprints, then oversee the project from inception to completion. They are present at the groundbreaking, and at the ribbon cutting. The same methodology applies to IT architecture. The IT architect is responsible for the design of the IT infrastructure environment, and is there from installation to testing to go live. The similarities between IT architects and others in the realm of architecture are striking. Now, with an understanding of what an IT architect does at a high level, let's dive further into their role and why they are important.

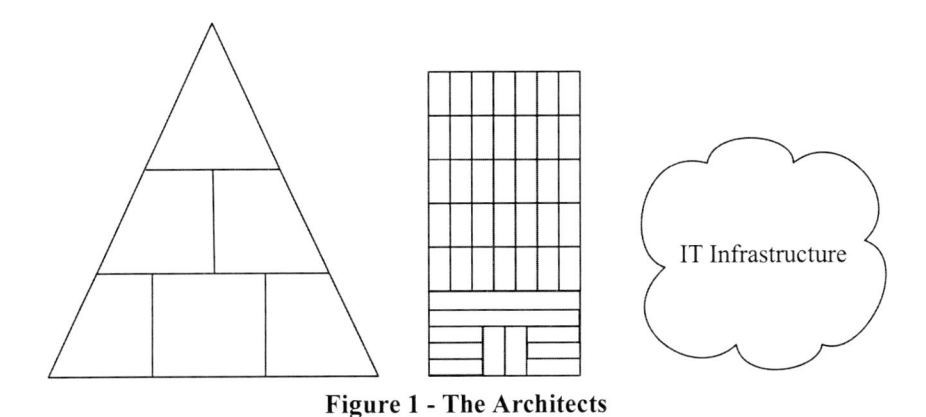

Figure 1 - The Architects

The IT Architect

Some people frown at the use of the word architect for IT architects. While these seasoned professionals may not create buildings, they have vital roles in today's world. Technology impacts almost part of our daily lives, and almost everything we do.

Let's take a typical workday. One usually starts by waking up, getting dressed, and going to work. This daily routine can be accomplished without technology, right? Well, **it depends**, of course. Did you turn on the TV to check the latest news? Did you unlock your smart phone to clear any notifications or check your schedule for the upcoming day? If you did, you have leveraged an IT environment painstakingly designed, configured, and brought into production by IT architects. What if you did not do any of these things? The home you live is consuming some sort of utility such as electricity or gas, and guess what? That electric company supplying resources to your address depends heavily on its IT infrastructure in order to keep track of your consumption and bill you accurately.

Now, after you left your house, did you stop for coffee or breakfast? Whether you paid by cash or card, the transaction was recorded into a system designed by IT architects. If the place you stopped was part of a national or international chain, the specials of the day may have been communicated to the store using some sort of electronic process. This electronic process required an IT architect to design and build its underlying infrastructure environment. If you stopped by a local coffee shop, they still need to order inventory and pay their employees, which they may use an electronic system for. It could be as simple as logging into a website to do whatever they need to, but the website? It required an IT architect at some point in time. This website may be used by not just this local coffee shop, but many more customers depending on its architecture.

Let's take a step back. Wow. You have not even stepped into your office yet, where you will log into a computer to access systems created by you guessed it, an IT architect. IT architects are needed everywhere today, and we cannot go about our daily lives without touching a system they have created. It may not be the Great Pyramid, but it sure is impressive.

What Makes an IT Architect?

So, the question remains, what makes an IT architect? This is one of those questions that you will almost always get a different answer to depending on who you ask, but from my experience, I have determined it boils down to several things:

Passion

While the job of an IT architect may seem to be revered and glorious from the outside, the truth is it is laborious, demanding, and time consuming. Many have an image of someone in a cape, swooping in, and swooping out, all while leaving a fully functional system behind them. If it seems this way to you, you have probably observed a skilled IT architect with years of experience. However, it is not as simple as it seems. Being an IT architect means working cross-functionally with many groups inside an organization, from the users, to the business owners, to the engineers. This is not always smooth, as different groups may have different needs and different requirements. It is up to you, the IT architect to help these unique groups refine these requirements, and ultimately provide a solution that meets them. This may entail long hours, listening when you may really want to speak, and paying attention to even the smallest details.

IT architects are passionate about providing the best solution they possibly can to their customers. They are also passionate about bringing different groups together, and finding commonalities between different areas inside the organization. Passion is needed to get you through the trying times, when obstacles arise, or when it may seem like a project is going to fall apart. A little bit of passion goes a long way.

Have you ever sat in a meeting or lecture where the presenter did not seem to care about what they were talking about? I would be willing to bet you lost focus quickly. The passion you exude as an IT architect is contagious to the others involved in the project. Everyone around you will thrive on your energy, and it will bring people together.

Humility

The best IT architects are clearly proven experts in their field, there is no doubt about it. The best IT architects and can also relay their ideas to others without belittling them or making them feel inferior. We have all seen the **smartest person in the room syndrome** in action, and we have all cringed. If an expert, or someone else involved in a project is making you feel like an idiot, chances are you are going to ignore what they are saying and tune them right out. It is just in our nature as human beings. As an IT architect, you do not ever want to be the person who is belittling others and getting tuned out. You are the IT architect, and you are in that room for a reason. You have nothing to prove to anyone.

Along with humility comes patience. You will meet people who may not understand what you are trying to accomplish. Maybe it is the storage guy sitting in the network meeting, but your job as an IT architect is to ensure all your customers understand the solution you are proposing. This may require explaining concepts repeatedly, or putting in extra time to ensure everyone is comfortable with the evolution of the process.

At times, you may find opposition to your work as an IT architect. There may be a time where you drop the hammer, so to speak, on someone who refuses to agree with you. Eventually you will encounter the person who refuses to even listen to design choices and justifications. This person can still be addressed in a humble manner. As you progress during your IT architecture journey, you will see practicing humility will serve you much better than leading with a pompous attitude.

Experience

One of the things you need to become an IT architect simply cannot be substituted, and this thing is experience. Experience is crucial to an IT architect, for many reasons, and it is not just one type of experience. Of course, you will need technical experience in a number of areas, but one area often overlooked is experience with people, and the softer skills needed to become an IT architect. Being an IT architect is just as much about gaining experience with softer skills, such as people skills, as it is technical experience, which we have briefly touched on.

This is the part where you are probably starting to cringe, but please do not. Experience is the easiest thing for you to get as you start your journey to becoming an IT architect. During the course of this book, I will be sharing how I gained experience during my IT architecture journey. You will be able to apply the methods I share you with to technical skills, as well as the softer skills needed to become an IT architect.

There is one more important thing you will need to become an IT architect.

Knowledge

If you are going to be an IT architect, you need to know what you are talking about! While knowledge and experience go hand and hand, they are not quite the same. Think of knowledge as being familiar with something. Experience is more along the lines of knowing what to do with this something. This is especially true when it comes to technology. For example, I may be able to read a ton of documentation about a storage array, and understand it works on its own, but I may not have the experience to know how to configure it, or know how it interacts with other areas of the infrastructure.

As I mentioned, knowledge and experience are the easiest things to get, but they require both passion and humility. Passion is needed for the time and energy you are going to need to put in to learning about various areas of architecture. Humility is needed because this is not going to be a solo journey, you are going to need help from others to get farther down the road. If you have never asked anyone for help before, the time has finally come, and it can be a difficult thing to do.

What Does an IT Architect Know?

Now, after discussing some qualities of an IT architect, we must ask ourselves the next question. What is it that IT architects really know?

Technology

Well, this one is a no-brainer. An IT architect must know technology, after all, IT does stand for Information Technology. This is the easy part, believe it or not. We will talk more about learning new technology in a coming chapter, but you are going to need to take more than just the technology with you on the journey.

There are many aspects of the technology an architect is familiar with. Many times, I will hear negative comments about IT architects because they are not **hands-on enough** or did not know a specific setting off the top of their head when it comes to a certain technology. One thing important to note is IT architects need to have a broad view of the technology they work with, especially how these technologies interact with the rest of the IT architecture they are designing. Every IT architect has had hands on experience at some point in time, and how much of that continues with them along their journey is a personal decision everyone must make for themselves.

As for not knowing a specific setting off the top of your head, that is something which can be looked up on the Internet quite easily, and should not be used to measure anyone's skillset. Chances are you can find better uses for your time than memorizing lists of values or settings, unless of course, you are studying for some sort of certification exam. Chances are you will not remember what you crammed into your brain in a week anyway when it comes to committing the information to memory long-term. We will talk about this more when we speak about certification in a coming chapter.

As IT architects, we are concerned with every technology our customers could use to enable their businesses. I hope you find many customers who see technology as something they can use to gain a competitive advantage in their industries. While some of this may vary from industry to industry, there are many technologies which are universal across them.

The main technologies you are going to become acquainted with on this journey are as follows:

- Server and Compute
- Virtualization and Virtual Machines
- Network
- Storage
- Applications
- Backup and Recovery
- Business Continuity and Disaster Recovery
- Security

You will be seeing this list quite a bit, and we are going to dive deeper into these technologies soon. It is impossible for me to give you an exhaustive list of every technology you will encounter along the journey, but this is a good core list to get you started. I will also call out several technologies that I think you will encounter sooner rather than later during the course of your journey.

The Softer Things

Besides technology, there is also a much softer side to IT architecture. You are going to have to be good with people, because you are going to be dealing with them quite a bit. You will be working with customers to determine things like what their requirements are, as opposed to what your customer may think they are. You will also spend time with them learning about how they operate their current IT infrastructure. Besides just speaking with them to learn about their organization and environment, you will also be presenting to them on topics like the IT architectures you create for them, technologies new to their environment, and ways to improve their existing processes. This softer side of IT architecture is something often overlooked. Once again, it is impossible to list out every single skill you are going to need when dealing with each and every customer you encounter along the way.

Along this journey, we will spend more time talking about this softer side of IT architecture, and how to develop your skills in these areas. When we talk about these softer skills, we are going to focus on the following:

- Gathering Requirements
- Determining Constraints
- You Know What They Say About Assumptions
- Identifying and Managing Risks
- Project Planning
- Procurement and Vendor Management
- Public Presenting and Speaking
- Written Communication

This list is a great starting point to build these skills during your IT architecture journey. After we talk about how to gain these technical and softer skills, I hope you will be able to apply the learning methods we talk about to other skills further down the path of becoming an IT architect, and in the journey we call life.

Your Customers

You are going to see me use the word **customer** quite a bit during our journey. I know many of you may be tempted to discount this, or skip ahead when you see me use this word since it does not pertain to you if you do not work for a vendor or partner. After all, you are a customer of many IT vendors, right? Of course, but there is something else which is very important to remember. At the end of the day, you have customers too. Your customers are those who rely on your infrastructure to run their applications, so whether you work for a vendor, partner, or a traditional IT customer, you have customers too. I will use the word **customer** to describe who we are creating IT architectures for, no matter where we work or what our role is today.

You may encounter IT architects who seem to stick with the same type of customers over and over. For example, they may deal with mainly healthcare customers because there are some specific requirements that specific industry has, and they are well versed in them. Of course, this is a path you can follow, or you can choose to work with many different types of customers. The key is for every architect to gain a good understanding of the customer they are going to work with or are currently working with. Every organization has its unique quirks, no matter what the industry. You can work with two different pharmaceutical companies, and have them be vastly different in the technologies and processes they follow.

What You Don't Know

An IT architect needs to understand what they do and do not know, so they can gain the knowledge and the experience to know it! While this may seem like a simple task, it can be quite difficult, so do not worry about it if your eyes are glazing over when you take a look at some of the technology and soft skills we are going to be working with. This is an important area on the journey to becoming an IT architect, and we will talk more about it in a coming chapter.

How to Find It

So now that you have figured out what you do not know, how to you go about learning it? There really is no easy answer to this question. We have a lot of learning ahead of us, and more importantly, we have got to learn about learning! A big part of this journey is figuring out how to gain these skills, especially if they are not in your day to day job description. In the coming chapters, we will dive into this much deeper.

How to Engage the Right People

As I mentioned before, this is not going to be a completely solo journey. Besides you and me, you are going to have to engage others whose expertise you seek. You are going to have to leverage your passion and humility in order to get help from others, which can be difficult for some. There is a good chance if you want to be an architect you are a highly driven self-starter that is used to being able to do anything they want if they put their mind to it. While that works for most things, it is not a substitute for experience, especially the experience of others. You can learn a lot from what other people have done before you, especially from their mistakes and successes.

More Than Just This Journey

We are going to dive deeper into these things during the course of this book. While I am sure you are fascinated about how I became an IT architect (or not, that is okay too), this book exists for much more than just telling my story. This book is going to be your guide along your personal IT architecture journey, and I am here to help you.

I also want this book to take you much further than just this journey. When we talk about different methods of learning these various skills, my hope is the knowledge you gain here will follow you on your next journey, wherever that may be.

The Use of the Word Architect

While we, as IT architects, have an awe and respect for our architect counterparts, sometimes they do not feel the same way. While we use the word architect with respect and reverence, there can sometimes be legal connotation to this. In some places, you must have a license to call yourself an architect. We do, however, meet the requirements of the word **architect** by definition. According to the Merriam-Webster dictionary, an architect is "a person who designs and guides a plan or undertaking". This is exactly what we do as IT architects, and why I will be referring to us as IT architects during our journey.

Please be sure to find out the requirements for the use of the title of architect in your locality. We would not want you to get in any trouble.

Before We Go

The journey to becoming an IT architect is not a journey with a set length or time period. The journey is different for each and every one of us, since we all have unique skillsets at the beginning. A big part of the journey is going to be asking ourselves questions. Some will be easier, but some are going to be much harder to answer. We are about to start asking ourselves these questions, and we are going to start with the harder ones first.

Do I Want to Be an IT Architect?

This is the first question we are going to ask ourselves. It is a very good question, and the only one who can answer it is you. You may have picked up this book knowing for sure you want to be an IT architect, or maybe IT architecture is something which you find interesting, but you are not sure about pursuing. You may also be curious about what an IT architect knows and does.

If you know you want to be an IT architect, fantastic! You have come to the right place, and this book will be your guide along the way. Knowing where to go next in your career is half the battle. Today's world is full of endless possibilities, which can be overwhelming at times. A career path can go in so many different directions, and it can be hard to decide which path to take next.

Not everyone knows what is next for them at any given moment, especially if they have recently achieved a big goal. You may have gotten a big promotion, and it may have been in the works for years, and now you are wondering, "What is next?". It may take time for you to figure out what the **next big thing** is for you.

This brings me to my next point. If you are reading this book and you are not sure you want to be an IT architect, do not put it down! This book can help you decide for sure if IT architecture is for you or not. My goal is to teach you some important lessons which can be applied to more than just IT architecture. You may finish this book and decide IT architecture is not quite the thing for you right now, or maybe even ever. You will, however, know the role an IT architect plays, and this may help you in your own career by being able to lead a discussion with an IT architect to ensure you get the solution your business really requires.

Next, we are going to talk about something that can help anyone, regardless of the path they choose to ultimately follow.

CHAPTER 3
SELF-ASSESSMENT

"The only true wisdom is knowing you know nothing."
— *Socrates*

When an architect is faced with a new challenge, they must first research the problem before solving it. If an architect is seeking to apply a certain style to a skyscraper when they are used to working with residential houses, there will be work to do before they even begin drafting. It takes a professional to admit they need to improve on some of their skills before starting a new venture. One of the hardest things to do is to be critical of yourself sometimes, but it is essential before you begin your architecture journey. There is only one direction from here, forward, though we need to figure out where it is we are going.

Honesty Is the Best Policy

If you are serious about becoming an IT architect, the time has come for brutal honesty. The only way you will be able to improve upon your skills is if you are honest with yourself about where your weaknesses are. If this is giving you a sick feeling in your stomach, there is a silver lining, you do not have to share this information with anyone but yourself.

Why the big push on honesty? It is for your own good, I promise. The last thing you want to do is to be in a position where you do not know something when you really need to. Of course, "I don't know." or "Let me research that further and get back to you." are both valid responses from an IT architect. However, it is crucial to have a fundamental understanding of technologies you will be using. If your customer starts talking about their migration to a leaf-spine network topology and you are thinking of apple trees and skeletons, you are going to have a really bad time.

The Self-Assessment

Now that we are being honest, it is time to take a critical look at our skill set and why we are here. Let's start with what we are doing here in the first place. I want you to ask yourself some tough questions, and be honest with yourself. If you look at Appendix A of this book, the Self-Assessment Workbook, you will find a workbook I have created to help you begin the journey. After you finish reading this chapter, this workbook is a place for you to perform your own self-assessment. I also highly suggest getting yourself a journal to record your journey in, which we will talk more about after we have finished the self-assessment.

Why Are You Beginning This Journey?

So, what brings you here in the first place? We have talked about how architecture is not all glory. What is driving you to begin this journey? Are you curious about how infrastructure components interact with each other? Are you looking to provide an end to end solution for customers? Do you love to solve complex problems? If you said yes to these, and came up with even more reasons why you are interested in beginning the journey, I am thrilled. You are even closer than you ever imagined to becoming an IT architect.

Now for my unpopular opinion on becoming an IT architect. I have mentioned the qualities you need to become a successful IT architect, and for me, it has always kept coming back to passion. Several years ago, I learned a very important lesson. Life is precious, and life is short, so it should be lived to its fullest. This lesson includes being happy and fulfilled in all areas of your life, both professional and personal. If you are not passionate about IT architecture, you should not be going down this path. Find the right thing for you, and begin that journey.

There is another driver I did not list above, and is often cited by those wanting to become IT architects…money. Is IT architecture a premium skill set which deserves to be compensated accordingly? Absolutely! This does not mean you should be in it solely for the money. After all, your happiness is worth more than any job could ever pay you.

What Do You Want to Do?

So, once you become IT architect, what do you want to do with your newfound knowledge and skillset? This may not be a question you can answer today, but it is something you should be thinking about during the process. If the answer is "I don't know.", do not worry, it is quite alright. Later in this book, we are going to talk about IT architecture skills in practice, so you may find some inspiration there. A good way to start this brainstorming process is to write down some of the technologies you enjoy working with the most right now. From there, you may be able to target what you want to do as you travel a little further down the road.

Where Do You Want to Go?

This is similar to the question you just asked yourself, but with a twist. Where do you want your IT architecture skills to take you? With anything, there is a what and a where. You may already have an idea of what you want to do already with your newfound skill set, but you may not know where you want to do it quite yet. If you are not sure, do not worry, you have plenty of time to figure it out during the journey. Take a few moments to outline where you think you may want to go, be it a specific company, industry, or even a new team in your new organization.

What Are Your Skills?

Now for the biggest, most complicated question of all. What steps do you need to take to begin your journey to becoming an IT architect? What are the skills you need to work on during this journey? This question, like many of the questions you will be faced with as an IT architect, does not have a simple answer. I will, however, walk you through the process of answering it for yourself. Now it is time to honestly assess our skills in the various areas of IT infrastructure. I am going to guide you through how we are going to be performing our assessment, and then you can evaluate your own skillset by using the Self-Assessment Workbook in Appendix A.

IT Architect Series: The Journey

Skills Assessment for Technology Skills

We are going to start with technology skills, since believe it or not, these are the easiest to come by. If we are looking to put together an end to end IT infrastructure solution, what areas do we need skills in? First, let's talk about how we are going to measure our skills, on a scale from one to five.

Table 1 - Skill Assessment Guidelines

	Rank	Skill Description
Low Skill	1	I can spell it.
	2	I have a vague understanding of it.
	3	I can hold a decent conversation on it.
	4	I have a good understanding of it, and feel comfortable working with it.
High Skill	5	I can teach someone how it works.

If you rank yourself a 1 in a category, you can spell the technology and you know it exists. If you rank yourself a 5, you are really good with the particular skill, so good, you would have no problem teaching it to someone else. Do not be afraid to rank something as a 1, in fact, do not be afraid to rank more than one skill as a 1. We all have at least one area we are unfamiliar with when we are starting our journey. Maybe we were never exposed to it in our career, or we simply did not find the areas interesting (until now, of course). This does not mean you will never be able to become an IT architect, it just means you will need to work on some areas a bit more than others.

Now, as an IT architect, let's think of the technology areas you should be ranking yourself in. I like to call them the infrastructure areas of expertise, since some of these areas may have multiple technologies within them.

- Server and Compute
- Virtualization
- Network
- Storage
- Applications
- Backup and Recovery
- Business Continuity/Disaster Recovery
- Security

If you do not believe me when I say you should know about all these areas within an IT infrastructure, stay tuned for a later chapter. We are going to talk about why every one of these areas are relevant to your skillset as an IT architect.

The Self-Assessment Workbook will guide you through the assessment for each of these areas. You can also download a copy of the Self-Assessment Workbook on the *IT Architect Series* website. Here is a sample skill assessment for virtualization:

Table 2 - Sample Technology Skill Self-Assessment

Skill Name: Virtualization
Current Skill Level: 1☐ 2☒ 3☐ 4☐ 5☐
Goal Skill Level: 1☐ 2☐ 3☐ 4☒ 5☐

Here is an example of how to determine your current skill level and goal skill level for a technology. Let's pretend I am working as a network administrator, and I have heard a lot about virtualization. I am always configuring the switches for these VMware ESXi hosts. Their network requests are not terribly complicated but there are more and more requests coming to me each year, so I know this technology is pretty hot right now. Last year, Michelle from the virtualization team was nice enough to explain the basics of this technology to me when I was working on one of her requests, and it seems interesting. I want to be able to have a good understanding of how it works, and feel comfortable working with it. I am not quite sure I want to become a VMware master yet though, so I am going to say I want to move from a skill ranking of two right now to four later.

As an IT architect, you should strive to get these skills to levels four and five. Some may argue you must be a master in all the areas of technology you will touch, but I do not think this is a realistic expectation. There will be some areas infrastructure areas you are not quite as passionate about, so you may be miserable trying to spend a good portion of your time and effort there. You do, however, need to have a good understanding of the technology, and how it works. This is also an important reason why teamwork between architects can be extremely important during an engagement. A customer may choose to bring in several different IT architects to work together, based on their individual areas of expertise.

The Self-Assessment Workbook will guide you through the assessment for the topics we have outlined in this chapter, as well as provide you with a few blank tables for anything else you may like to improve on.

Setting Goals

Now since we have determined where we are and where we want to go with our skills, we are going to create some goals for the technology areas we know we need to improve our skills in. The process of setting goals is a life skill you can use far beyond the journey to becoming an IT architect. First, let's look at a sample goal. We are going to continue our example of wanting to become more proficient with the technology of virtualization.

Table 3 - Sample Goal for Technology Skill Development

Technology Name: *Virtualization*		
Today's Date: *January 1, 2017*	**Goal Completion Date:** *July 1, 2017*	**Time to Complete:** *6 Months*
End Goal: *Be able to install and manage VMware environment. Also understand how VMware works.*		
Top 3 Things I need to work on: *1. Learning how VMware works (What runs on a VMware ESXi host? What does VMware vCenter actually do?) 2. How does VMware impact storage and networking? 3. What are some common issues during operation a VMware environment?*		
Other Things I Want to Learn: *How to use things like PowerCLI for administrative tasks.*		
Issues I think I may encounter and How to overcome them: *I need to build a home lab environment, so that will require research. I am also not a VMware person, so I want to see if Michelle from the VMware team at work will spend some time with me explaining some of the operational aspects of the environment.*		
Revisions:		
Goal Met Actual Date:		

As you can see, I have identified some of the key things I want to learn about virtualization, and any issues I think I may encounter during the process. There is also a space for my revisions as I go through the process, and a spot for the actual date I meet my goal. Let's face it, life happens. Sometimes a project comes up where a million hours a week is not enough time to work on it, or something in your personal life will need tending to. I believe in striving to meet your goals in a timely manner, but it will not always happen this way.

This may seem like a silly exercise, but there is something powerful about writing down your goals, and placing them in a visible location you will see every day. You may want to place a sticky note with some of your current goals someplace you will be sure to see it over and over again. Now, you will have something tangible you can look over on a regular basis versus an abstract concept dwelling in your mind. Writing down goals like this is your first step in becoming an IT architect. Congratulations!

Sometimes I find I can be a little too ambitious when I initially set a goal, which I know is going to be the case for many others as well. In today's world, almost everything can be at your fingertips in an instant. Why wouldn't these skills be there too? At some point on the journey, you may become discouraged. This is a normal part of the process, and I encourage you to focus on how far you have come instead of how far you have left to go. Sometimes switching to learning a new topic can give you the boost you need to get back on track.

The best thing you can do for yourself is to continue to be honest during the learning process. The important thing is to recognize early on that your goals will evolve along with you. This will help prevent you from becoming discouraged if you see your timelines slipping, or when this little thing called life impacts the timeline of your journey. I would encourage you to check in on yourself on a monthly basis to see how things are going, and if you need to revise anything in your plan.

Skills Assessment for Soft Skills

Since we now understand what our technical skills are, let's move on to the next area we will need to work on as an IT architect. We have talked briefly about these other skills, beyond just the technology you will need to become an architect. I like to call them soft skills, or the architectural building blocks, which are the true foundation of an IT architect. The technical skills are simply layered on top. Soft skills are also the trickier skills to gain experience in. While you can read a book on many of their concepts, the best way to get experience with these skills is to get exposure to them, which we will talk about soon. What are these soft skills anyway? They are skills such as:

- Gathering Requirements
- Determining Constraints and Assumptions
- Identifying and Managing Risks
- Project Planning
- Procurement and Vendor Management
- Public Presenting and Speaking
- Written Communication

Some may not find these skills very interesting, and may even cringe after reading this list. While many of us in the IT industry tend to gravitate towards our technical skills, the fact remains technology is only one small part of IT architecture. These soft skills can be even more important than the technology you are working with. A big part of IT architecture is using our technology skills in conjunction with our soft skills, such as using a particular feature to solve a business problem.

If you still do not believe me, we will dive more into why these softer skills are so important soon enough.

Our trusty Self-Assessment Workbook has a section for you to assess your skills in each of these areas, as well as goal sheets to help you devise a plan for areas of self-improvement. This is similar to the process we already walked through for technical skills.

Let's use the example of project planning.

Table 4 - Sample Soft Skill Assessment

Skill Name: Project Planning
Current Skill Level: 1 ☒ 2 ☐ 3 ☐ 4 ☐ 5 ☐
Goal Skill Level: 1 ☐ 2 ☐ 3 ☐ 4 ☒ 5 ☐

When working on a project as a network administrator, project managers assign tasks to me to accomplish by a certain date. One of the project managers I often work with, Matthew, always makes sure I feel the timeline is reasonable for what I need to accomplish. Other than that, I am not sure how the overall process works. I know this will be important during my architecture journey, so I am going to speak with Matthew and see if he has some guidance for me. I do not necessarily want to be a master project manager, but I want to be able to perform the function if needed.

Now, it is time to fill out a goal sheet for this skill, just like we did for the technology based skills we wanted to learn.

Table 5 - Sample Goal for Soft Skill Development

Technology Name: *Project Management*		
Today's Date: *February 11, 2017*	**Goal Completion Date:** *June 11, 2017*	**Time to Complete:** *4 Months*
End Goal: *Be able to perform the duties of a project manager, and have a good understanding of how a project runs from start to finish.*		
Top 3 Things I need to work on: *1. How to coordinate resources across teams.* *2. How do I estimate the time it will take to perform a certain task?* *3. What are the different phases of a project.*		
Other Things I Want to Learn: *How to handle items like resource constraints, and when equipment does not arrive on time.*		
Issues I think I may encounter and How to overcome them: *This is not really something I do in my day-to-day job. I am going to ask Matthew if he would be willing to spend a few hours with me and explain the process. I am also going to see if I can shadow him in some of the other meetings he has about the project we are working on together.*		
Revisions:		
Goal Met Actual Date:		

As you can see we followed the same process as we did with our technology based skills. The goal setting process works for technology skills, soft skills, and any other skill we want to develop, even the fun skills we are going to cultivate during our IT architecture journey. Goal setting is something to take on every journey you go on, not just your IT architecture journey.

What Does Success Look Like for You?

Since we have talked about our goals, let's talk about our ideas around meeting them. We all have different views of what personal success is. As you start meeting with your customers, and determine their requirements, you will start to get a handle on how they see success. Right now, I want you to start thinking about what a successful journey to becoming an IT architect looks like for you. This is a question which will require some thoughtfulness to answer. You may not even be able to answer it until you get a bit further along in your journey. It may be gaining a certain number of skills, or getting a new job. It may also be meeting your goals within a certain time period.

Whatever it is, for you, be sure to keep thinking about it and take a moment to write your thoughts on it in the Self-Assessment Workbook. Just like how it is important to re-visit your goals, it is important to revisit your ideas on success.

Before We Go

Before we get really get started on our journey, I have some general advice for you to keep at the front of your mind. When you are feeling stressed out, or like you are not making enough progress fast enough, come back here and review this advice again.

A Word on Time

Time is a funny thing. Sometimes, it feels like you have blinked, and an entire year has passed. Other times, a year seems to drag on forever. When we talk about the journey to becoming an IT architect, we are talking about embarking on a journey that can take a great deal of time, usually measured in years. Becoming an IT architect should not be confused with obtaining an expert or architect level certification. Obtaining a certification can happen much more rapidly if you have the underlying skills it requires. We will talk more about certifications in a later chapter.

So how long does it take to become an IT architect, then? This question has a different answer for everyone. As you begin your IT architecture journey, you will realize most questions asked of you share the same answer: "It depends.". The time it takes you to become an IT architect will depend on many things such as work commitments, personal commitments, how much you need to learn, and the people you meet along the way. If you set a hard goal such as "I want to be an IT architect in five years.", you might be disappointed if the goal takes longer to achieve.

Burning Out

If you have not yet experienced being burnt out in your career, you are incredibly lucky! Unfortunately, there will come a time when you will experience this wretched event. There is a good chance you will not do anything to trigger it yourself. You may be tasked with an insane deadline requiring you to work 80 hour weeks. If you are working on IT architecture skills when they are not a part of your daily routine, your journey will add to your already hectic schedule and you will burn out even faster.

I do not what this to happen to you, which is why I am emphasizing re-evaluation and revising your goals along the way. This journey is meant to be a learning experience, and dare I even say, fun! Adding more to an already full plate will not help you in the long run, it will probably just make things worse on all fronts. Remember, there is no set time limit on this journey. It is as much about what happens along the way, as it is the end result.

If you feel yourself heading towards burning out, and believe me, you will know it is coming if you have not experienced it, make sure to take a step back for a moment and evaluate things. If it is work related, there is probably nothing you can do to relieve it, but you can make it more bearable. One tip I have learned is to schedule time for yourself. It can be something small, such as making time each day to read a magazine, read a chapter in a book, or draw. This should not be related to your job or IT architecture journey, it is meant to give your mind some time to rest and recharge. If you do not feel like you can do this, I encourage you to start with something such as ten minutes a day. Set your alarm ten minutes earlier, or stay up ten minutes later at night to do something for yourself. For me, it is always the latter option (I am not a morning person!).

To help you along, there will be a goal sheet for developing a fun goal in the Self-Assessment Workbook. I really encourage you to pick something for the goal which does not relate to your IT architecture journey. When you need a break from your journey, this fun goal will be there so you can change your focus for a little bit and refresh. I have found if I take a break from something for a while and come back to it, I often return to it with a fresh perspective. This fun goal will also make you feel like you are making progress while you are resting your IT architecture muscles, which will be a win-win for some of you who always like to focus on moving forward.

Failure Is Not an Option

There is another reason people are sometimes hesitant to begin this journey, the fear of failure. Chances are, if you are really good at one particular area of IT infrastructure, you have not failed at anything lately. Let me tell you a little secret you should always keep in mind. There is no such thing as failure.

Wait, what? That is right. Read that sentence again. There is no such thing as failure. Sure, we all mess something up once in a while; after all, we are only human. As you learn and broaden your skillset, yes, these things will happen, and sometimes they will not be fantastic. The key when something like this happens is to learn from the experience, and I do not mean to beat yourself up over it endlessly. Take the opportunity to assess the situation and determine alternative possible outcomes when things do not quite go your way. As long as you learn from something during the process, you have not failed at it.

Now we have taken an honest look at our current technology and soft skills, and set some goals. Let's continue our discussion on skills, this time focusing on the ones which will help you learn new things.

CHAPTER 4

LEARNING NEW SKILLS

"There are no great limits to growth because there are no limits of human intelligence, imagination, and wonder."
— Ronald Regan

The pyramids were not built in a day. Neither was Rome, or much else for that matter. While a great deal can be accomplished in a single day, and everyone has those amazing productive days, you cannot become an IT architect in a day. Even if you have already mastered many of the skills you are going to need to become an IT architect, you will still come across things you need to learn during the course of the journey. In fact, any IT architect will tell you, the world is still full of things they still want to learn, no matter what they currently know. Learning a skill is a skill within itself, and once you figure out the combination of learning methods which works best for you, all you will need is time.

Methods of Learning

Everyone has their preferred methods they use to learn something new, and you may already have an idea of what your preferred method of learning is. I want to cover different methods to learn things in general, before we dive into learning specifically what you need to know as an IT architect. After we talk more about what the architectural building blocks and infrastructure areas of expertise really are, we will talk about techniques for learning new skills in those areas specifically, while developing our existing skills.

Even if you think you already know how you learn best, trying out different learning methods for gaining new skills diversifies your brain to absorb new information. Beyond the technical and softer skills we will pick up on our journey, a new way of learning can be a great way to further enhance the skills we already have. The fact of the matter is, you will have to use most of these methods on your journey in some way shape or form, so let's get acquainted with them now.

Learning by Seeing

Are you the type of person who just looked at an equation on the board in calculus class, and it made perfect sense? If so, I envy you. Some people learn best by seeing something. This method can apply to many things, such as watching someone solve a calculus equation, or watching the way a tool is used. A person who learns this way may be ready to give it a go themselves, after all, they have already seen it done.

YouTube is the greatest invention in the universe for people who prefer this learning style, and I think we all have a little bit of this learner in us. I am sure you are thinking about a time where you watched a video on YouTube and tried something which was anything from a technical skill to a new recipe for dinner. In this day in age, there is more than likely a video for any of the things we are trying to learn on our own.

Learning by Hearing

Maybe it is not seeing an equation written on the board, but hearing the words spoken while it is being written. For some, a complex task can be simply explained verbally, and they are ready to go out there and do it.

YouTube is great for these people as well, since you can play a video in the background and listen to what is going on, provided the audio track explains things thoroughly. Audio books and podcasts are also a great platform for these learners to pick up new skills, especially if you do a lot of driving, or have a long commute. If you have a 30-minute commute to work each way, you can easily utilize those 5 hours a week to absorb new content.

Learning by Reading

For many, nothing substitutes a good book. If you were the person in school that read the chapter being covered that day in their text book before class, then spent the period working on your homework for another subject, you are probably this type of learner. Sure, it is nice to have someone explain things, but you would rather spend your time diving into a book yourself.

Various electronic devices are great for this purpose. There is always a dedicated eBook reader or whatever your electronic device of choice is (whether it be a phone, tablet, or computer) to use to store your reading material. If you find reading on a tablet or computer screen bothers your head or eyes, an eBook reader which uses eInk may be the right solution. By using eBooks on your device of choice, you can carry an entire library with you wherever you go, which is a very powerful thing in itself. Here is a tip from my own experience: make sure you disable notifications on the device you are using during reading time, or you may find yourself distracted and not getting very much reading done at all.

As much as I love to read, and have many books at my fingertips, there is nothing like the feeling of a good paper based book. These days, I reserve this honor for the subjects I am most interested in only, or I would need a dedicated library to store my collection. I will also reserve it for the topics I find more difficult to learn. I have noticed even a slight change in the way you are consuming the material can really make the knowledge you are reading stick.

Learning by Doing

It may not click for you until you do it yourself. When we talk about technical skills, this learning method will be a big one. Some people just need to configure something once on their own to really solidify the concepts behind it, and the understanding of how it really works. For others, a quick configuration here and there just does not do it. These people just want to set something up completely from soup to nuts, which I think everyone should try to do at least once with every technology they work with. There is nothing like stumbling your way through a technology for the first time to get your mind really working.

The good news? With today's technology, most of this is within your reach, as long as you have got a trusty computer as a sidekick. A computer is going to be one of your most important tools during your IT architecture journey.

Learning by Teaching

I am a big believer that you fully understand a concept when you can teach it to others. If you can go from zero to hero, and bring along others for the ride, you may be this type of learner. You may use combinations of other learning methods to plan your lessons for others, which is great reinforcement of the concepts you are teaching.

If you are seeking to create a pre-recorded demo to use during a lesson, this will also combine learning by doing, and help you solidify those skills further. Sure, you could also do your demo live, but make sure you really know what sort of environment you will be teaching in. The last thing you want to have to do is try to connect to a remote sever without having an Internet connection. This also applies for presentations and demonstrations to your customers.

Learning Alone

Some people love their solitude, and enjoy sitting down, working on something, and mastering it. I have encountered many people in the technology field who absolutely love to learn alone, and I am included in this group at times. Many of us have gotten into this field due to our natural curiosity about how things work, and why. We also tend to be tinkerers, which is something we can do by ourselves just fine.

The ability to learn on your own is a useful skill. You will not always be surrounded by like-minded people when you have the time to work on some of your skills. Since there are many opportunities out there for us to steal just enough time to learn a little something, anything you can work on alone will be a benefit to yourself.

However, there is one thing which is difficult to figure out on your own, the **real-world** perspective on the things you are learning. For example, let's say I am reading a book on VMware vSphere, and how to configure an VMware vSphere ESXi host. I cannot even begin to tell you how many ways there are to skin that cat, but let's say you are trying to apply a host profile to your ESXi hosts to configure them. In this case, you have 77 ESXi hosts, in three clusters. Sure, you can apply the host profile to each of the 77 hosts, 77 times, or you can attach it at the cluster level, and be done with your task after applying the host profile three times. If you do not have a lot of experience with ESXi, you may not know to use the more efficient method of applying host profiles. Tidbits like this are the things you can pick up for experts who already have a great deal of experience with the technology you are learning. The experience of others will be one of the most invaluable assets on your journey to becoming an IT architect, which brings me to my next topic.

Learning with Others

I have noticed learning with others does not always come naturally to some in the technology field. If you have never been a part of a study group before, the journey to becoming an IT architect is the perfect time to start. No matter what learning method you use, there is someone out there who already knows what you want to know. If you are lucky, you may be able to find them, and they may be willing to teach you. This is a learning method I promise you will use during your journey to becoming an IT architect.

I think some of you are going to cringe. Not everyone enjoys working in teams or groups. After all, we must do it all day every Monday through Friday as part of our job. We remember those all-nighters pulled either in college or our career to meet a deadline that the rest of the team did not pull their weight on. If you do not like learning with others, it just means you have not found the right people to learn with yet. **A group of like-minded people seeking to learn the same thing can be an unstoppable force.**

For some of those who learn best by teaching others, you also may enjoy learning with others. Think of a local user group meeting you have attended in the past. If you have not yet attended one, now is the time to start. Presenters are excited about the topics they are speaking on, since the topic was something they were seeking to learn about at one point. They want to share their knowledge with others. Some of the best conversations and learning also happens over coffee or in the hallways of these events.

The Socratic Method

Since we have spent some time talking about how valuable it can be to learn with others, whether it be by teaching or forming a study group of aspiring IT architects, I want to mention the Socratic Method. This method, was of course, created by Socrates himself. Much of what we know about Socrates we have learned from the works of one of his students, Plato.

The Socratic Method is an interactive learning method. The leader of the discussion provides information and asks questions which make the learners think. Sometimes, the questions may be leading, and may challenge you to say no to the teacher, and explain the way it really should be done. This is a fantastic learning method which can be very helpful in study groups, or even in business situations. I encourage you to research this method further, and see how it can be applied to your journey. I will remind you of this in the Resources Appendix.

As a teacher, Socrates was not much a fan of the lecture. Yes, even back in ancient times, the equivalent of a boring PowerPoint presentation existed. This is something we can all relate to. At some point or another, whether it be in academia or business, we have all been stuck in a horrible lecture. Can you tell by the number of times I have said **horrible lecture** I really do not like horrible lectures?

As a learner, I like to be engaged. To me, listening to someone read slides has never held any value. After all, I can read slides myself, probably much faster than whoever is reciting them to me. There is nothing worse than material you thought would be interesting presented in a boring manner. This just makes you lose interest in the presentation you would otherwise be excited about.

While I had many great professors in my academic career, one sticks out in particular. He was the head of the Electrical and Computer Engineering department, and every single class he taught was interactive. He would ask **us**, the students, questions. I would go out of my way to try and take a class with him, because I knew it would be engaging, and I would learn a ton.

My absolute favorite lecture I have ever attended in my life was by him. It was an Electrical Engineering class, and he led us through a discussion which led us to determine Electrical Engineering is the best major ever, because there is not anything in today's world that can be done without it. It still sticks in my mind today, because of the way he approached it using the Socratic Method.

Before We Go

Before we really start learning by using these different methods, I have some more tips for you. I really want to help you get in the right mindset as you are beginning your IT architecture journey.

Find A Mentor

This, of course may be easier said than done. Your employer may have a mentorship program already, so try and take advantage of an already existing program. If there is not, or you are not excited about the formalness of the program, you should look for someone whose abilities you respect. They do not need to be an IT architect necessarily, but it will not hurt if they are. A mentor is someone who can push you when you need a push, and see when you are struggling and give you advice and a shoulder to cry on (there is a good chance there will be tears of some sort on this journey, so don't say I didn't warn you). They should share your drive and determination to continuously improve themselves, and those around them.

Remember, a mentorship is a two-way relationship, like any other. This is someone who is donating their precious time to help you better yourself. It will also be a rewarding experience for your mentor, as long as you respect their time and abilities. Now is not the time to be the smartest guy in the room, now is the time to listen and absorb. Each mentorship relationship is unique, so it will be up to you and your mentor how your relationship is structured. Above all else, always make sure you are prepared for your meeting with your mentor. If not, it would be wasting two peoples time instead of just your own.

You may have difficulty finding a mentor at work. If you work for a smaller company, chances are you may very well be the go-to person on the tech side of things. Even at a large company, you may be the go-to person when someone is trying to solve a technology problem. You may have people who just are not interested in being a mentor, even if you could learn a great deal from them. If you your place of employment is not yielding you a mentor, do not worry, there are many other options. A great place to start is with your local user groups, which you can find more information on in the Resources Appendix. You will probably meet people there who have already begun the journey, and are more than willing to help you get started.

While a mentor can help guide you in many areas, there is one thing they cannot do. They cannot do the work for you. This is a conversation I have had with my mentor many times. One of the reasons we get along so well is we are both driven people, and hard workers. As my career progressed and I joined the vendor side of the house, I was very lucky part of the onboarding process was being assigned a mentor. I was even luckier my mentor was nothing short of amazing. He taught me the ropes as I assimilated to vendor life, and he is a big part of how I have gotten to where I am today.

A big part of the success of our mentorship was because he was willing to teach, and I was willing to learn. I saw the opportunity of having a mentor with a great deal experience in an industry which was brand new to me, and made the most of our time together by listening to his advice. As I learned, our mentorship changed. Instead of him giving me suggestions on how to handle situations, I would turn to him with ideas to handle them, and he would talk through them with me. I truly hope everyone is lucky enough to have a mentor like this.

While a mentor may guide you, and help push you along, do not expect them to hold your hand the whole way, or give you a trophy when you fall flat on your face (which may also happen during the journey). Even with a mentor, this journey belongs to you and you alone. Think of a mentor as a member of your support team, they will hand you a bottle of water, but they will not run the race for you.

Start A Blog

A blog is a great way to record what you are learning during your IT architecture journey! For example, sometimes I will write a blog post on a tip or certain feature of VMware, then reference it later when I cannot quite recall how to do something. A great example is when I am looking for a very specific line of VMware PowerCLI code I know I have written before, but am not getting quite right from memory. Your blog can become your resource for remembering these details, and it also help others with their learning.

Building a library of these tips for yourself is a great way to get started blogging. It does not have to be much, there are many free blog services out there if you do not want to mess with managing much. Blogging is also a great way to flex that writing muscle, a skill we know we are going to need along our journey. Remember, your blog does not have to be the prettiest, and you do not have to have 2,000 word blog posts, but if that is the sort of thing you are interested in I am not stopping you.

Blogging can also be used to relax, especially when frustration arises with a certain topic. Stuck on a networking problem? Why don't you try researching a storage tidbit and write about it? VMware ESXi giving you a hard time? Stuck on writing a certain document? Go blog on anything you want.

Your blog also does not have to be technical. Sure, technical blogging will help you hone some of those skills, but feel free to write about something else completely different. The goal of starting a blog is for you to practice writing and learn something. There are so many topics out there in the world, do not feel like you are constrained to just one.

Get a Journal and a Planner

There is no better way to make yourself feel good on a down day than to look at how far you have come in your journey. I highly recommend getting a journal and a planner, and to make sure to specifically record activities related to your IT architecture based learning. It can be as simple or as fancy as you want. Getting a journal does not mean you have to spend a lot of money on something fancy. I am a big fan of those marble notebooks, or just any blank notebook for many of the projects I work on. When I worked on my VCDX certification, I had a blank sketchbook for drawing diagrams and brainstorming, and a lined notebook for notes during the process of writing my submission. Then, when I started preparing for my defense prep, I started a new lined notebook to make sure that material was easily accessible. These notebooks were great tools, because it was easy to flip through them and see how far I had progressed, and I knew I could just grab a notebook and review it when I had enough of looking at a computer screen. I filled almost all three of those notebooks.

While notebooks are great for recording things and brainstorming for sure, there is also something to be said about a paper-based planner. Now you may live and breathe by the calendar on your smart phone, but it is nice to try to lay out a daily, weekly, or monthly plan for a specific goal (then again, we know what they say about **best laid plans**). There are so many planners out there, again, it could be anything, even another regular old notebook or calendar. You can always draw in whatever views you would like to use (monthly, weekly, daily, etc.).

The goal of this planner, however you purchase it and create it, should be tracking your activities as you progress during the journey. For example, if you plan to work on a technical skill from 9:00 PM to 10:30 PM at night, go ahead and block that out in your planner. I also like to put notes in my planner on the tasks I worked on, as well as listing other related tasks to complete, or ideas on what to research next. Visualizing it this way will help you make your studies a habit during the journey. You can also pick one day a week to decide what topics you will be working on when, and update your planner accordingly. In this case, it can be a great guide for you when you are very busy, simply look at your planner to see what time you have reserved for studying, and what topic you will be working on.

This is not the only way to use your planner. Something else I frequently do is use planner space for a to do list. I also recommend picking yourself up a pack of colored pens, pencils, or markers. For example, I may not have anything scheduled from 6:00 AM to 9:00 AM in the morning, so I will make a colored box around that time, and write out my to do list there. I will use blank space for brainstorming, and use a different color to make boxes around those ideas.

Paper planners really have made a comeback in the last several years. Social media is full of pages dedicated to showing off planner layouts, and you can use these to get ideas on how to best use your planner. My general rule of thumb is if there is free space, I should use it for something. If you do not like the paper based idea, I encourage you to try to do the same with an electronic planner.

A Whiteboard is a Fantastic Tool

Sometimes, it helps to have space to draw a concept out. A whiteboard is a great tool for this. Your whiteboard does not need to be expensive or fancy. I bought a roll up whiteboard on the Internet for about forty US dollars when I was preparing for my VCDX defense. I stuck it to the wall at home. I also brought it with me on my trip for the defense. I rolled it back up and put it in my suitcase, then stuck it to the wall in the hotel room. This was a great tool for last minute preparation. Do not forget the markers, either!

Whiteboarding is also an important tool as an IT architect. You will often find yourself drawing diagrams on a whiteboard for your customers. Believe it or not, this is a skill which takes time to develop. The best advice I have is do not talk into the whiteboard, talk to your customers. It may take you some time to figure out the angle to write at to accomplish this, and it will take some practice to make your diagrams legible while talking and drawing at the same time.

Before I got my roll up whiteboard, I bought a pad of easel paper. This tool works well when you do not have space for a whiteboard. You can practice the same skills you would on a whiteboard, and save some of your drawings as you progress. The smaller form factor is also good to practice with since you may only have an easel in some customer situations. While you can save pages from your easel pad, I also recommend taking pictures of your whiteboard when you feel you have created a great diagram.

Get A Computer

Well, this seems like a no brainer. Sure, you could write an IT architecture document on a smart phone, but that does not mean you should. A real keyboard will be an excellent tool for you along the journey, as will a mouse, as simplistic as it sounds. Everyone should have a computer, preferably with some power to it. Whether you prefer desktops or laptops, something with at least 16GB of RAM is easy and cost effective to come by these days. This computer can also serve as a lab for you to test out your new technology skills with various simulators and virtual machines.

There is a fantastic section in the book *IT Architect Series: Foundation in The Art of Infrastructure Design* on building a home lab, and many, many blog posts out there to help get you started. Some people have better home labs than most small businesses, which is an amazing feat. This does not mean you need to buy a rack of equipment for your basement. A good laptop or desktop is enough to get you started with some desktop virtualization software like VMware Fusion, VMware Workstation, or VirtualBox. This will allow you to virtualize different infrastructure components and run them all on your computer, creating something called a nested home lab to help you on your journey.

Find A Friend

If you do not know anyone who is looking to become an IT architect in your day-to-day life, I encourage you to sign up for Twitter! It may sound silly, but it is a fantastic way to meet like-minded people who have the same goals. The best part about this is there are no geographic boundaries. If you meet someone from the other side of the world who is looking to learn the same topic you are, you just need to worry about figuring out what time zones you are both in. A friend along the journey is a great way to challenge yourself and can be a great sounding board. If you need that extra push sometimes, a study partner is a great way to get it. Social media is also a great way to find a mentor if you have not been able to find someone to mentor you in person.

If you are not quite ready to share your journey with the world, that is alright too. However, it is certainly something to think about as you progress. It can also be helpful if you are focused on a certification, but we will talk about that in a later chapter.

Picking Out Our Walking Shoes

Before we go, I want to talk about a few more things to keep in mind during our journey. As with many other things in life, there is no substitute for putting in the work. I really want to draw some analogy to practicing a sport and practicing a new skill, but I have to be honest, sports were never my strong suit, so let's go back to focusing on putting in the work.

The journey to becoming an IT architect will not be a nice paved path. There are going to be hills and valleys, and some rocky terrain too. There may also be spots where you cannot even see the path, and that is why you are reading this book. Together, we will be able to navigate any obstacle we come across during the journey. Some parts of the journey will be a casual stroll, and others will be a fight up the side of a mountain.

When you are hanging off the side of the mountain, make sure you review the goals you have set for yourself, and how far you have come. This is one of the reasons a journal is a great idea. No matter where you find yourself on your journey, remember, it is just putting one foot (or hand if you are climbing) in front of the other. No matter how slow you feel you are going, you are still going faster than those not attempting to complete this monumental journey. Focus on what drove you to begin the journey in the first place, and use it to help you through these rough patches.

Now that we are armed with some new methods of learning, we are getting closer to putting in the work we are going to need to do in order to become an IT architect.

CHAPTER 5

ACADEMIC AND PRACTICAL IT ARCHITECTURE

"The saddest aspect of life right now is that science gathers knowledge faster than society gathers wisdom."
— Isaac Asimov

If we follow our analogy of constructing a building, there are a number of different ways architects can be trained. Often, there is some sort of academic training, as well as a great deal of practical training. If you look at projects like creating a skyscraper glimmering in the sunlight, the lead architect most likely did not just finish a degree program. An intern or fresh university graduate may have contributed to the building, but skyscrapers are not built by those with no practical experience. There are too just many things which need to be learned before that level of a project can be undertaken, and these things take time.

Academic Architecture

The academic world is an interesting place, especially in the IT world. There are many who scorn academia all together, since it just is not their thing. On the other hand, some revere it. There are also many who fall somewhere in-between.

Before we continue along this track, I want to make something perfectly clear. You do not have to have an academic background to be an IT architect in any way shape or form. However, academia and IT architecture do have a very interesting relationship, which you may still be interested in. I promise, this chapter is worth your time.

Now that we have gotten that out of the way, let's continue along.

You Can't Go to University for IT Architecture

While you can go gain an undergraduate architecture degree if you want to design buildings, the same simply is not true for those who want to design IT environments. The major does not exist, and in my opinion, it absolutely should not.

I have to admit, I am one of those slightly academic types. I hold both a Bachelor and a Master of Engineering (yes, Engineering, not Science!), and I worked very hard to get them. I am also extremely proud of them. As an undergraduate I trained in classical engineering, one of the hallmarks of the Bachelor of Engineering degree is they put you through the paces in all the specialties of engineering, before you spend time with your own. While I focused on Electrical Engineering, I gained an exposure and understanding of all the variations, as well as hands-on design experience in each area.

I was 17 years old when I started my engineering program, and 20 when I finished. While I had a fantastic understanding of engineering, my understanding of how things happened in the real world was not as strong, even though I was an IT infrastructure intern on Wall Street during my studies. I also had half of my Master of Engineering degree completed, which had very different types of courses than my undergraduate studies, so I may not be the best example of a fresh-faced, clueless engineer without any experience.

Let's continue with this example though. Imagine I did not have any hands-on experience at that point, and I had to rely only on my academic training. Electrical Engineering does not address anything remotely about IT infrastructure, neither does Computer Engineering, Computer Science, or any major you could choose at the undergraduate level. There may be a stray networking class, or class about how databases work, but that is as far as you are going to get. The undergraduate level is more about teaching methods of thinking and problem solving, than it is about teaching about the specifics you are going to encounter during your career. A university degree can give a foundation for your career in the technology industry. Your first job after completing a degree is your opportunity to learn how things are done in the real world, like an apprenticeship.

The Graduate Level Teaches You Enough to Be Dangerous

During the courses of my Master of Engineering Degree, I took a couple of network architecture courses. Remember how I wanted to be a network architect back in those early days? I focused on Secure Networked Systems Design, which was a mashup of network design, general systems design, and security. Because I liked to make myself suffer, I also took some electives in IT strategy and management.

At that point, I did have a decent amount of network experience, and I had already gotten all that "What does a router do?" stuff out of the way. The way we looked at network design was along the lines of "Can we connect this stuff and make it work right? Can this router talk to this switch, and how does it need to be configured to do so? How do we troubleshoot it when it breaks? How do we measure and ensure performance?". All things which are very important to a network architecture, but still missing some very key components as I know them to be now. There was little discussion of meeting customer requirements, and little to no focus on enabling a customer's underlying business.

I will say some of the IT management and strategy courses did fill in part of the gap. However, these lacked integration with actual technology. It was more of the soft stuff, like how to talk to other business units in an organization, and how an IT organization was structured, which was sort of funny in itself, which I will get back to in a moment.

There was not much that put these things together. The only reason I got any sort of remote exposure to the business side was because I put myself through it for fun. Graduate programs are often focused on the business, or the engineering, but seldom both. I was lucky to attend a university that allowed you to mix and match the two programs.

The Real World Is Your Trial by Fire

Even those of us who are academics often tend to roll our eyes when we encounter a recent graduate at any level, who seems to think they know everything. As we know, when you are younger, you feel invincible and you do think you know everything for the most part. It is not until we grow a little bit we realize this is not quite the case.

This is also why you see many companies with recent graduate programs. They realize the academic world and the real world are vastly different, and they are trying to guide those recent graduates along in getting some real-world experience.

I entered such a program after my undergraduate degree. It was the pilot program for the company I went to work for, and it was…interesting to say the least. Let's just say it had its challenges and leave it at that. The goal of the program was to have the recent graduates rotate through four different areas of the information technology areas over a two-year period. This is where I got a little sidelined from my goal of becoming a network architect, because I ended up on the team which was handling this cool new thing called virtualization, but I digress.

I finished my Master's degree during this period, and I quickly realized that some of these IT management classes were not set in the real world. They were preaching what an IT organization should be, while I was living my life in something completely different. While that part of the course did not do much for me, I was able to extract some valuable skills from it, mostly in how to work across different units of an IT organization. These are the types of lessons which are universal, and you can carry to any IT organization you end up being a part of. A big part of being an IT architect is studying your experiences, and learning from them. Remember, winning is winning, and failing is learning.

Gradually, You Become an IT Architect

If you look hard enough, you can in fact find graduate level courses in IT architecture. Quite honestly, you probably do not need them once you have got some experience under your belt. As you learn and grow during the course of your career, you will find yourself evolving and looking at things differently. We will talk about how some of this translates to becoming an IT architect a little later, but most of your evolution will not be learned by reading a book, it will be learned by watching others and by doing.

If your journey has been from undergraduate work, right into a graduate course of study, even if you take courses on IT architecture, you will still need some experience under your belt before you can truly take on an architecture of your own. No matter how many degrees an IT architect may have, real world experience is still a crucial aspect to their training. Many enterprise architecture courses add an element of role play to attempt to simulate the customer interaction and experience. Any enterprise architect can tell you this simply will not cut it. Without experience in the real world, you will never encounter the situations which are just way too outrageous to be real (and yet, they are, and you have no choice but to deal with them). Whether they will admit it or not, every enterprise architect has at least one of these stories.

Theoretical Versus Practical Skills

When we talked about different methods of learning, we covered a great deal of ground. As we continue our journey, we will get further into the specifics of how to apply these methods to different skills. I will give you a little bit of a spoiler alert now, we are going to be talking about a number of different ways to get practical experience in some of areas we need to work on.

We have talked about why academic skills do not amount to everything, and this can also apply to reading books, white papers, and other technical documents. When I talk about gaining skills like this, I am going to call them theoretical skills. Sure, I could read a whitepaper on a Cisco Nexus 9000 switch, but does that mean I can go become a network architect, or even engineer?

Of course not. There are so many nuances you will only pick up by getting some practical and applied experience with this sort of technology. Don't get me wrong, I love a nice white paper, in fact I read them all the time. All the time! There is probably not a day that passes where I do not read some sort of technical document I did not create myself. Why? Being an IT architect is more than just knowing technology at a single point in time, it is about evolving your skills along with the technology. This is why we are going to focus on building both our theoretical and practical skills during our journey.

Now back to our discussion on these types of skills, and why they are both so important.

Following Worst Practices

There are some interesting things you will come across as you delve into white papers and other technical documents. One of these things is something vendors like to call **best practices**. Most IT architects would lean towards calling them worst practices instead. Not necessarily because they are bad advice, they can be very helpful to an IT architect, but there is something missing from a vendor generated best practice. Nowhere in any white paper or best practices guide will you ever be able to find anything about your specific customer's requirements.

Best practices are more of a generalization than a rule. They are usually developed by very skilled engineers. I am not saying best practices are not relevant when making a design choice, because they may be. Unfortunately, no matter how skilled, the engineer who developed them has no idea what you are walking into with **your** customer. Blindly following these best practices can quickly lead you astray.

Let's take the case of the brand-new hypervisor, SuperUltraExa (I just made it up, it does not exist, unless some venture capitalist is reading this and wants to give me money). In the SuperUltraExa best practices documentation, it says to enable jumbo frames. Now, if we read the SuperUltraExa documentation, it does not say we must have jumbo frames, it just says they may increase performance.

Jumbo frames are Ethernet frames with a Maximum Transmission Unit (or MTU) larger than the standard size of 1,500 bytes. When we put more data in a single frame, by increasing the MTU size, or enabling jumbo frames, we have the potential to allow the SuperUltraExa hypervisor host to process more data at a time. Ultimately, it will process more data, but fewer frames.

Now, as the new SuperUltraExa administrator, you turn on jumbo frames on the switch inside your hypervisor host. Things go haywire. Your IP based storage keeps disconnecting. You start seeing performance issues, and stuff just does not work right. Was this not a best practice from SuperUltraExa directly?

Yes, but they did not tell you the actual impact of enabling jumbo frames on the SuperUltraExa virtual switch. If you are going to be using jumbo frames in one area of your infrastructure, you need to enable it end to end. Sometimes you may be setting the MTU to 9,000, but do not forget about the header for the Ethernet frame. Your network devices may need a higher MTU to account for this. You will also need to make sure your network switches, your virtual switches, as well as your hypervisor host's Network Interface Card (NIC) are all enabled for jumbo frames. This is one of those little things which has probably burned almost everyone once when they have started out in the IT infrastructure world. Your customer may have been hurt by it too, and will not even entertain the idea of enabling jumbo frames in their environment. So much for following the SuperUltraExa best practices!

This is just one example of how you need to be able to extrapolate from a vendor's best practice, versus adhering to it blindly. Let's say you want to use SuperUltraExa's revolutionary new feature, LightSpeedSync, which provides synchronous replication at any distance. What if your storage vendor does not recommend the use of LightSpeedSync because it makes the storage arrays run at a higher utilization? This may not mean you do not use LightSpeedSync at all, it just may mean you need to keep a closer eye on your storage arrays and size them accordingly, since you have business requirement driving the use of this feature.

As an IT architect, it is your job to come up with the best practices for **your** customer's environment. Sure, you may use some best practices from various vendors, but you may develop your own to suit your customer's unique needs. You may not have the ability to do this until you have gotten a bit of applied experience with some of the technologies you will be working with as an IT architect.

Enterprise Architecture Frameworks

Now that we have talked a little about best practices for technology, let's move to our next topic of discussion, enterprise architecture frameworks. Some may think these are the same as best practices, but for enterprise architecture instead of a specific technology. This is not quite the case.

Think of a framework as an approach to thinking. When you follow an enterprise architecture framework, you are following a methodology, not strict guidance. An enterprise architecture framework will not tell you specific technologies, or a specific order of implementation. They will take a holistic look at the organization, and how to approach infrastructure design within it. They also will not tell you the steps to get to a completed design from A to Z. Enterprise architects do not simply follow a check list, they understand there will be things unique to each customer, based on the way the IT organization operates.

I go back and forth on frameworks. Sometimes I think they can be helpful and useful, and other times I find them to be hindering. When we think of being an IT architect, we are focused on technology. What many do not realize until they start the journey is there is an art to IT architecture as well. As you do more research on enterprise architecture frameworks, you will see some key tenets they share. As an IT architect, you may follow the key tenets, but put your own twist on it. This is where the art of infrastructure design comes in. You just cannot simply create a cookie cutter design and re-use it with every single customer if you want to truly meet their business-driven requirements. A great resource during your IT architecture journey is the first book in the IT Architect Series, *IT Architect: Foundation in the Art of Infrastructure Design*.

There is not one framework to rule them all. My recommendation to aspiring IT architects is to start by looking at two different frameworks. The first is called the Zachman Framework. The Zachman Framework will challenge you to see the enterprise architecture from different viewpoints. This is especially helpful during the journey, as you begin to discover what customers are looking for from an IT architect. The CEO is going to have a very different view than the virtualization engineer, or the CTO for that matter. As an architect, you will need to create collateral relevant to each of these different roles within an organization. The Zachman Framework will help get you into that mindset.

The second I recommend researching further is TOGAF. This is a little different than the Zachman Framework, as TOGAF is maintained by an organization called The Open Group. TOGAF goes a step beyond the Zachman Framework and will also outline specific tools for IT architects to use. TOGAF provides a detailed outline of what IT architects should be concerned with, for example, in security. The goal of The Open Group is to create a true standard for IT architecture.

Both of these are worth picking up a book or another resource on. Even if 100% of these frameworks do not resonate with you, they are more than worth understanding as part of your IT architecture journey.

Not Those Kinds of Models

You are going to be doing a lot of reading and research on your journey. Whether it be framework related, or about architecting a specific technology, you are going to come across three main models: the conceptual, logical, and physical models. You sometimes hear them referred to by different names, but the core ideas are the same. They can also have different contexts, and be applied to different areas. Let us briefly talk about what they are.

Conceptual Model

We are going to pay more attention to this later, but when you think of the conceptual model, think of something you would be presenting to a CXO type resource. At this grade, the people you encounter usually will not be concerned with the low-level details, such as what port a server is plugged into, or even the specifications of that server. We will dive deeper into the conceptual model a little later, but if you were to illustrate a conceptual overview of an environment, it would look something like this:

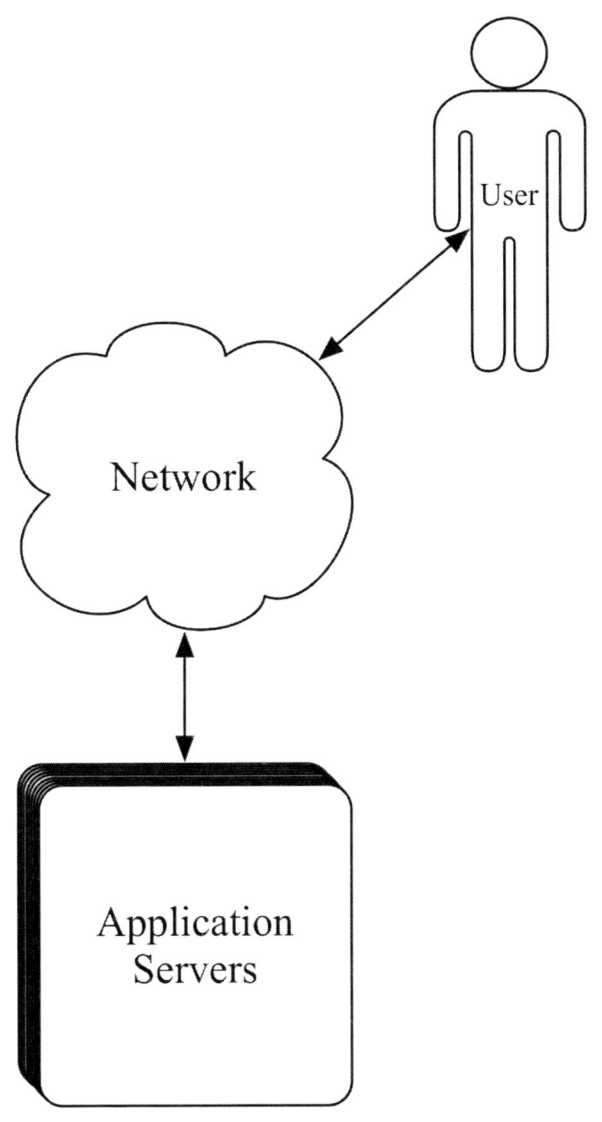

Figure 2 - Conceptual Diagram

Logical Model

As IT architects, the logical model is where we are going to spend a great deal of effort. In fact, this is the model IT architects are usually the most concerned with, and where they do the bulk of their work. At this point, we still are not mentioning specific vendors or technologies. If the logical model is done correctly, an IT architect should be able to switch out vendors at the physical level in the eleventh hour, with the design still meeting all of the customer's requirements. For example, as part of a logical design, you may be deciding if you are using rackmount or blade servers. However, you will not be determining the vendor you are going to use at that point. Sizing of various infrastructure components is also a logical activity, but again, you will not be determining which physical model of hardware meets these calculated values until you begin working on the physical model. Consider the logical model as defining required the technical and operational capabilities.

Let's take a look at a logical diagram of a server connecting to a network.

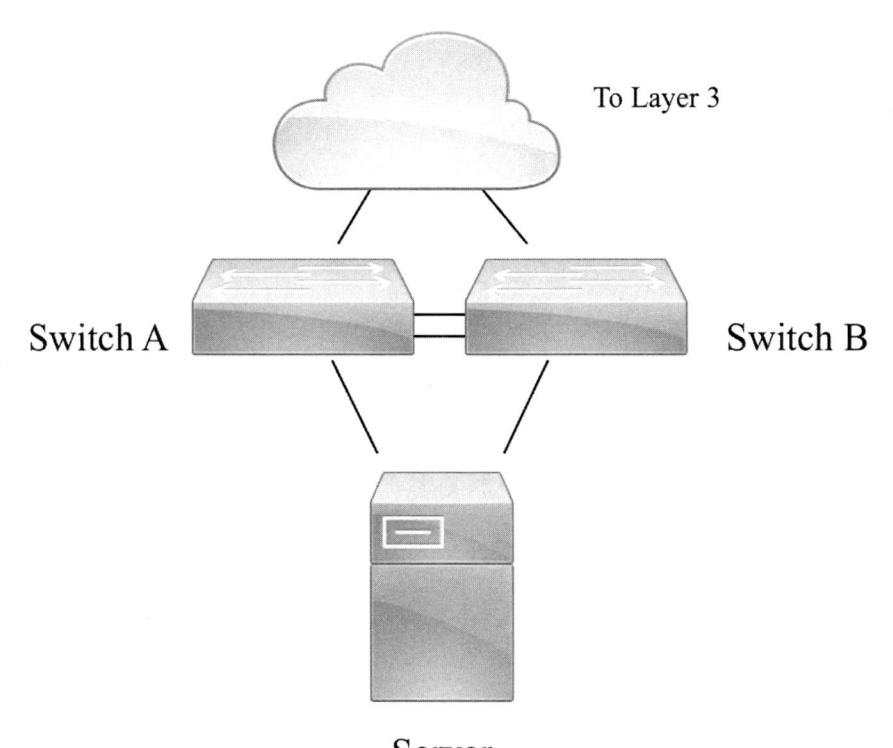

Figure 3 - Logical Diagram

Physical Model

The physical model is the specific detail of how the solution is put together. In this model, we are mentioning things like vendors and models. We are showing what ports get connected, and what protocols connect them. This is the view that the engineers implementing the solution and running the solution really care about. Consider the physical model to be the manifestation of the logical model technical and operational capabilities, specifying vendors, products and configurations.

Remember our example before, of connecting a server to the network? This is what the physical representation would look like.

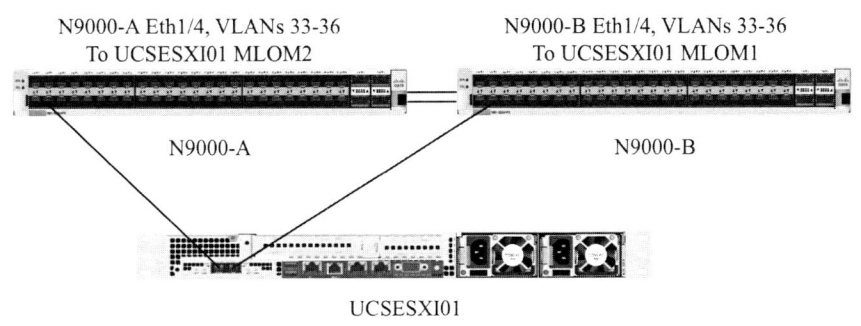

Figure 4 - Physical Diagram

As you can see, we are connecting Cisco C220 M4 servers to Cisco Nexus 9000 Switches. The physical model is very different from the conceptual or logical models, but it is just as important.

Why This All Matters

As an IT architect, you will be delivering a conceptual design, a logical design, and a physical design based on these models. It is very important to show the progression of the architecture you create. Do not forget, you will have to explain your architecture to different members of the organization, and they may all be concerned with different areas. An IT director may be concerned with the conceptual and logical designs, but the storage manager may be concerned with the physical design. These can be considered viewpoints or levels at which a person in a particular role looks at the design, metrics, and configurations. Remember our friend Zachman I introduced you to earlier? I highly recommend reading his paper "Conceptual, Logical, Physical, It Is Simple", and I will include a link to this paper in the Resources Appendix for you. Do not let the title get you frustrated if you do not find it simple after the first time you read it.

Chances are you are not used to working like this, and it may take some time to adjust. I am mentioning these models at this point in our journey together since they fit in that theoretical and academic type category for you right now. These are some of the hardest concepts to grasp as an IT architect, and they really require you to change your way of thinking. One day, a light bulb will go off in your head, and it will all make sense. I know, that sounds quite silly, but it is the truth. The more you work with these concepts, and start thinking in this manner, the easier it will become until one day, it all just falls into place for you.

Certifications

There are also a number of people out there that are not fans of certifications. I clearly am not one of them. What if I told you when I was taking networking classes at the age of sixteen I went through a little program called the Cisco Networking Academy, which were university classes which taught the material needed to gain the CCNA certification? Doing this would just double the pain and suffering for some. Some view certifications as measuring only **theoretical knowledge**, but it really depends on the particular certification and the particular testing process.

As you may already know, my big certification game so far was the VCDX certification and the VMware certifications leading up to it. Many, many times people questioned why I was bothering with a **silly certification**. For me, it was not something silly. It was a long standing personal goal I set for myself.

There is one thing I want to make perfectly clear, certifications are not the be-all end-all of proving you have a certain skill set. Sure, a certification may get you in the door for an interview, but you are on you own after that. A certification is only as good as the person who holds it.

If you are not a certification person, I am not going to try to make you become one. However, I would be remiss if I did not bring them up as a learning tool. The fact is, studying for a certification is a great way to learn new material. We will talk more about using them in this manner later, and I promise, you never have to take a test. Just keep an open mind.

Aspiring and Potential Architects

If you are still not sold on becoming an IT architect, I am glad you are still reading. If you are reading this book as an aspiring IT architect at the undergraduate or graduate level, I am glad you picked it up. The journey to becoming an IT architect is a long one, and as we all know, knowledge is power. The purpose of this book is to give you a better idea of what you will encounter along the journey, and how to navigate the rough terrain along the paths you take.

Before We Go

We have covered quite a bit in this chapter. While many of the things you will encounter along the way, from academic studies to technical white papers, to enterprise architecture frameworks will be great resources, they also can be a bit daunting at fist. While academics can be a huge part of an IT architect's journey, they are not explicitly required to begin it.

Remember, one of the hardest things about becoming an IT architect is to change the fundamental way you are looking at the problems you encounter. As an IT architect, everything becomes part of the bigger picture. As you read something like a technical white paper, I encourage you to think about how that specific technology will impact those it needs to integrate with to create an IT infrastructure environment. This helps us as we seek to transform our theoretical skills into practical ones.

Frameworks can also be a powerful tool, but can be confusing at first. I encourage you to take a look at the enterprise architecture frameworks we mentioned, but try not to worry about them too much at the beginning of your journey. As the journey continues, look back at them every once in a while. As you progress with the skills we have talked about, you will see things start to make more sense.

Finally, keep in mind it is very important to have both theoretical knowledge (which may have been gained from academia in some cases) and practical knowledge in the skills IT architects use. We are going to be talking a lot about these two very different skill types soon.

PART II
ON OUR WAY

CHAPTER 6

ARCHITECTURAL BUILDING BLOCKS

"Every great architect is - necessarily - a great poet. He must be a great original interpreter of his time, his day, his age."
— *Frank Lloyd Wright*

If you are an architect of buildings, you cannot just build a glass skyscraper every time you have a request from a client. The purpose of the building, as well as the land it is to be built on will play a big role in what you decide to architect. You will design a suburban home in a much different manner than an apartment building. You will also have to worry about ordinances and zoning regulations. It is not as simple as building the same towering glass structure over and over again.

While a big part of IT architecture is being able to put together multiple technologies to form a solution, there is much work to be done before we even touch a piece of technology. Being an IT architect is more than being good at putting together technology, it is about solving real world business problems for customers.

Architectural Building Blocks

One of the most difficult aspects of becoming an architect is training yourself to look at problems in a new way. For example, let's say a customer wants to protect a group of servers from hardware failures, and make sure they are also available in a second site in case something happens, like zombies, to the first one.

You are going to be tempted to jump straight to technology. I can install a VMware vSphere cluster in each site, making sure I have my VMware ESXi hosts configured in clusters and turning on VMware HA on in case one of those hosts fails. Then I can install VMware Site Recovery Manager, and make sure the virtual machines get to the second site. I am done, right? Sorry to break it to you, but you have not even gotten started. While the use of technologies may ultimately be what you use to solve this problem, but there are many more things which need to be done before this occurs.

Before we even think about technology, there is a number of architectural building blocks we need to learn and understand to become a successful architect.

The Bigger Picture

As an IT architect, it is very important to keep the bigger picture in mind. One of the most important things to remember is at the end of the day, you should be providing an end-to-end solution to your customer. Being an IT architect is not about putting together an infrastructure and walking away once you turn it on. It is up to you, as the IT architect, to lay out the plan from beginning to end for your customers.

To provide this type of solution, you are going to need some softer skills in many areas. We talked a little about what these skills are when we performed our self-assessment. These softer skills are:

- Gathering Requirements
- Determining Constraints
- You Know What They Say About Assumptions
- Identifying and Managing Risks
- Project Planning
- Procurement and Vendor Management
- Public Presenting and Speaking
- Written Communication

There may be some items in this list you were not thinking about when you decided to become an IT architect. This is not an exhaustive list of every possible thing you should understand as you continue your journey, but it is a very good starting point. Still not convinced these softer skills are important? Let's discuss them, and dive a bit deeper into what these skills really mean.

Gathering Requirements

Before you even begin to architect your design, you are going to need to begin the process of gathering requirements. Think of the requirements as the foundation of a building. You will not start to build the structure on top of it before the foundation has been poured and had time to set. The process of gathering requirements is often one of give and take, and can be one of the most arduous and time consuming portions of a project. Gathering requirements is also a lot like prospecting for gold, you never know when you are going to find a nugget of precious information. In an ideal situation, there will be a project kickoff meeting and various follow ups so you and your team can work with the customer and theirs to determine the real requirements of the project. During these meetings, be sure to pay attention to things like body language and nuances of speech, this will help drive you in the direction of those precious nuggets of information.

As an IT architect, you will learn which requirements you absolutely must meet from your customer to have a successful engagement. Most of these key requirements will link back to your customer's business requirements.

One of the things we are going to talk about from a technical perspective is Business Continuity and Disaster Recovery. While there are technical tools to accomplish this process, there are some very important business drivers which must be fed in.

Two of the most important things you need to know are your customers Recovery Time Objective (RTO), and Recovery Point Objective (RPO). Your RTO is how long it takes you to recover from a disaster, and you RPO is the point of time you are recovering to. Think of RPO as how old is the data you are recovering with. Also, tied together with these concepts is something called a Service Level Agreement (SLA). You have probably heard this term thrown around quite a bit, but it is important to understand what it means to your customer. The SLA will be measured in an amount of time, usually represented as a percentage of uptime in a series of 9's, such as 99.9% or 99%. The more 9's, the less downtime is tolerated. The following table translates the number of 9's a solution provides, and the allowed downtime.

Table 6 - A Listing of 9's

Availability	Downtime / Year	Downtime / Month	Downtime / Week
99%	3.65 days	7.2 hours	1.68 hours
99.9%	8.76 hours	43.2 minutes	10.1 minutes
99.99%	52.6 minutes	4.32 minutes	1.01 minutes
99.999%	5.2 minutes	26.3 seconds	6.05 seconds
99.9999%	31.5 seconds	2.59 seconds	.605 seconds

It is important to understand how your customer measures their SLA. Is the downtime allowed per year? Per month? Per week? As you can see by the table above, the answers to these questions can greatly impact the amount of downtime you need to architect for.

There are more questions you need to ask yourself as an IT architect. Does the SLA include planned maintenance? When is the SLA effective? Is it only during business hours, or is it 24 hours a day? These are all questions you will need to answer.

You may have different RTOs, RPOs, and SLAs for different tiers of service in an environment or for different applications. Chances are you will not be dealing with one set of requirements identically across the environment.

Why You Care

Your goal as an IT architect is to provide the customer a solution. Often, your success will be measured by your ability to meet the customer's requirements. Requirements are what will drive your design choices during the architecture process.

It is very important to ensure you are gathering your customer's requirements without any ambiguity. If the customer is looking for a **fast** connection between their sites, you need to ask follow up questions to determine what they are looking for. If they are asking you to pick server hardware within certain parameters, you need to understand why they are asking that.

There is almost never a situation where you will not be able to discuss a customer's requirements with them. Even request for proposal (RFP) situations generally have a method for asking for clarification on the customer's perceived requirements. Even after the RFP process, designs are often refined.

As for our RPO and RTO, we need to make sure they sync up with the customer's SLA, or we are going to have to prod them to do some more thinking on how their environment is truly run. Many customers will just want you to adhere to the SLA they have previously set in place, but you may find it impossible to do so with the RPOs and RTOs they have defined. This situation happens quite often, and it can be your expertise that saves your customer from a very bad situation.

You will also architect your environment quite differently based on these numbers. For example, if your RPO is one day, and your RTO is two days for a development environment, it will not be hard to achieve at all. If you only need your data from the last day, and your backups are replicated off site daily, you will be able to meet this RPO and RTO without issue.

However, if your RPO is 5 minutes, and your RTO is an hour for one of your most critical production applications, things will drastically change in the environment. The method you used to achieve the RPO of one day and RTO of two days will not work here. You are going to have to start looking at replication solutions that will be able to make sure your data is no longer than 5 minutes old. With this small window to replicate data, you will also need to make sure you have enough bandwidth. You will also need to ensure the replication of this data does not impact any other traffic on the same link.

This solution just became much more complicated, and much more expensive. Almost every customer would like an RPO and RTO as close to zero as possible, but there is a cost associated with this that not every customer is willing to pay.

What Could Possibly Go Wrong?

If you deliver an infrastructure which does not meet your customer's requirements, have you really delivered anything at all? While you may have done a ton of work, and spent a great deal of money and time on the project, the fact remains, if the solution does not meet your customer's requirements, you have not truly delivered a solution. There is just a bunch of equipment taking up space and making your customer's electrical bill go up.

Determining Constraints

Along with requirements, there is still more you will need to build your foundation. Next up are constraints. Think of constraints as things you have no control over, yet still impact the design choices you are going to make during the IT architecture design process. For example, if you need to leverage existing hardware or vendors, these would constrain your abilities to make design choices within those areas.

You will almost always have some sort of constraint. Some common constraints you will encounter are customers telling you to re-use existing hardware, leverage a recently added piece of infrastructure, or a pre-determined choice of vendor (or an exclusion of a certain vendor).

Why You Care

Part of your job as an IT architect is to explain why you have made the choices you have. To do this, you need to clearly understand what you do and do not have control over in the infrastructure. If you are told you must use an existing storage array, but your design calls for a new one, chances are the engagement may end early.

There are many people who cringe when they hear a customer wants to re-use something they already have. To those, I say where is your sense of adventure? Figuring out the puzzle is half the fun, and constraints merely challenge your thinking skills. Some of the most fun I have had as an IT architect is with constraints which forced me to think far outside the box. If every engagement let you architect an environment with new hardware with an unlimited budget, being an IT architect would not be any fun at all.

Speaking of budget, this can be one of the biggest constraints you deal with as an IT architect. Many customers are going to want an extremely fast sports car they can take to the race track, but they only thing they are going to want to pay for is a skateboard. It is up to you as the IT architect to translate their business requirements, and figure out what the customer truly needs. There may also be times where you have no choice but to go back to your customer and ask them to reevaluate their budget, you cannot very well build an VMware ESXi cluster out of popsicle sticks and bubble gum.

What Could Possibly Go Wrong?

Ignoring the constraints of an environment will not lead to anything good. If you are constrained by a 1-Gbps network, and you purchase 10-Gbps network adapter cards for your servers, you are going to be in deep trouble. It is important to meet the needs of your customer, and this includes keeping their existing environment in mind, even if it is not something you would choose to use in a design. Time to learn all about that software package you have dreaded forever, but your customer insists you use.

You Know What They Say About Assumptions

We all know what they say about assumptions, and it holds true in IT architecture. In an ideal world, there should be nothing you have assumed about an environment, because you have vetted everything out. There are some things you may need to assume which cannot be vetted because they have not happened yet. For example, at the beginning of an IT architecture engagement, you may have to assume hardware and software will be ordered with a certain type of support model, since these components of the architecture have not been determined yet, much less ordered. You will of course, validate this during the project, and you will clearly state these required components and support levels in your bill of materials.

There are times where a customer may tell you to assume things. For an example, a customer may tell you to assume they have 100 virtual machines, each with 4 GB of RAM, 2 CPUs, and 100 GB of storage for you to craft a response to an RFP. Even though the customer is telling you to assume this, you still need to document it and treat it with the care it requires. The chances are the customer is going for the classic **apples to apples** comparison. This will in no way shape or form resemble what you deliver at the end of the engagement. Part of your job as an IT architect can sometimes be to state the obvious.

Why You Care

Every IT architect starts with a list of many assumptions. Until you can do your due diligence, you have no choice but to assume some things. You will need to vet these assumptions during the architecture process, and eventually they will not be assumptions any more. If you cannot determine if an assumption is true or false, then it has the potential to become a risk, which we will talk about shortly. It is our job as IT architects to **minimize the risks we encounter**. As an IT architect, it is also important to clearly document your assumptions at every turn, so you, your customer, and your team remain in the same page.

What Could Possibly Go Wrong?

Assumptions can burn you badly. Let's use a twist on our example we talked about for constraints. If you walk into an environment and assume there is 10-Gbps connectivity, you could be in for quite the shock if it turns out they only have a 1-Gbps network, and the scope of your engagement does not include network upgrades. Or let's say you assume you have a certain level of licensing for VMware vSphere and go to town with distributed virtual switches…when you go to implement and you find out you did not in fact have VMware Enterprise Plus licensing, you are going to have a really bad day.

Identifying and Managing Risks

Risks are everywhere you go, in everyday life, and as IT architect. When we think of designing and IT infrastructure, there are different types of risks we must think about. Can the customer give me the exact details of a workload? If not, that is a risk. Am I constrained by pre-existing equipment? Depending on the equipment, it can also be a risk. If I pick a particular hardware model lacking in redundancy, that is a risk too. A risk can even be related to where the data center is located. However you look at it, there are going to be risks during the design process. Some will be inherent to the project itself, and others will be introduced as part of your design choices.

Yes, you read that right, you may introduce risk into the environment as you design it. It is up to you as the IT architect, to call these out, and have a plan for mitigating them. In some cases, you may need to come up with creative solutions to mitigate these risks. In other cases, the risk may be so inherent to the project, you cannot mitigate it. A good example of this is a customer with only one data center, and no place for offsite recovery in the event of a disaster. After all, you never know when zombies may invade the data center and eat your infrastructure.

For a much more detailed discussion on risk, I recommend reading *IT Architect Series: Designing Risk in IT Infrastructure* by Daemon Behr.

Why You Care

Risk Management is making sure your head does not roll when things go completely wrong, or when the **you-know-what** hits the fan. There will be times when you present a mitigation to a risk, and a customer may just not be interested in implementing it. The important piece here is that you document it as part of the design. This way, when the customer comes yelling that your solution failed them, you can point to the spot where they signed saying they understood the risks, and were not interested in mitigating them.

This does not happen very often, but it happens often enough to discuss it. The scope of a project can change quickly due to outside influence such as the company's financial performance, or business requirements to hit a certain date. These of course, all create risks for you to document and mitigate.

On the other hand, many customers understand risks are inherent to doing business, and are looking to mitigate everything they possibly can. If you point out a server you had to reuse has a single dual port 10-Gbps NIC card, they may be willing to spring for a second one, or keep several spares on site ready to go. It is up to you, as the IT architect, to document the possible mitigations for each risk in the project.

What Could Possibly Go Wrong?

If the data center is next to a known zombie breeding ground, and you do not document this as a risk, then the zombies are going to come for you after they finish eating your infrastructure (and possibly your customer). This is a silly example, but think of real world examples such as your data center being located in an area known to be impacted by natural disasters like hurricanes and tornadoes.

On the other side, if you are using a storage array without any high availability features, and did not document it as a risk, you can expect a screaming phone call in the middle of the night when that storage array fails, even if you were constrained by a pre-existing array.

Project Planning

While you do not necessarily need to be an expert project planner, you do need to have some ideas about how infrastructure projects run. Of course, there can be differences in the process based on what organization you are working with, but this is to be expected. To design a complete solution, you may have one large project with a number of phases, or the solution may be broken into different projects based on how the organization's Project Management Office (PMO) operates.

Why You Care

You cannot design a complete solution unless you can tell your customer how long it is going to take. You may even be up against time constraints. If you have three months to implement a solution, it may look completely different from a solution you have a year to implement. Understanding how all the project phases work together, and when they can be executed in parallel will be paramount to meeting your deadline.

What Could Possibly Go Wrong?

If your customer needs their infrastructure operational by a certain date, and you do not even come close to meeting it, expect major problems. Remember, IT infrastructure projects are driven by business needs, and if you cannot meet the customer's business needs you may not find yourself working with the customer very much longer.

Procurement and Vendor Management

Procurement and vendor management is something which can easily be overlooked when you are beginning your IT architecture journey, especially since procurement processes vary so widely from organization to organization. As an IT architect, you need to understand how the procurement process works for the organization you are designing an infrastructure for. This ties closely into your project management skills, as procurement can often add time to obtaining equipment.

Along with the hardware itself you may need to purchase, you are also going to need to purchase the software to run on top of it. You will need support contracts for the hardware and software, because let's face it, stuff happens. Sometimes vendors need to be called in for expert help, no matter how skilled the personnel running the environment are. Support is a huge aspect of procurement and vendor management, since support contracts may be included with the purchase of hardware or software, or purchased separately depending on the vendor you are dealing with.

Why You Care

You will need to understand how the organization will go about obtaining the equipment you need to build their environment. They may already have preferred partners and vendors they use. You will also need to know the impact of onboarding a new partner or vendor if necessary, as this can impact the length of the project. As such, you may even be limited to vendors and partners which are already in house to meet the project's timelines. Procurement and vendor management concerns should be flushed out during the beginning of the project, when you are gathering information such as requirements.

There may come a time where you are tasked to architect an environment using pre-existing hardware and software the customer has already paid for. You may think this gets a pass from dealing with procurement or vendors, but the fact of the matter is, you better make sure you have valid support contracts on everything you are using. Running critical applications without support on the underlying IT infrastructure is a very dangerous thing.

Now, let's not forget there are valid use cases for not having support. For instance, if new infrastructure has been purchased, the old, unsupported infrastructure may be delegated to the infrastructure lab. If you are up for buying parts from eBay and Amazon for the old stuff, this may be a very good use of equipment which does not have a support contract.

What Could Possibly Go Wrong?

Pretend you built six weeks into your project to obtain the server hardware you are going to need for your ESXi hosts. This may seem like a valid amount of time, but the vendor you selected does not have any sort of procurement contract with the customer you are working with. On top of that, the vendor has just informed you the equipment you ordered is back ordered. These are all things you should have flushed out ahead of time, and will make you miss the go live date you were planning for.

Public Presenting and Speaking

As an IT architect, you are going to spend time explaining your design choices. You will also be expected to be able to talk various people through the course of your IT architecture project. You will be dealing with everyone from operations, to administration, to management and executive level people. There are many ways to tell a story, and public presenting and speaking skills are something which are honed over time for every individual. You may also be sent to a by an employer to a user group or conference to speak. These skills will serve you well in any number of areas.

Why You Care

Public speaking is something that is daunting to many people. The thought of speaking to a crowd can induce panic, shaking, nausea and any number of noxious symptoms to the speaker. While these skills can seem particularly daunting to someone who does not have them, they are still extremely important. Public speaking and presenting skills also take some time and effort to sharpen, but more on that later. As an IT architect, you want to be able to present your design to whatever audience you need to. In some situations, your presentation may be one of the critical elements in a customer deciding if they are going to go with your design or someone else's.

Beyond all the ways this particular skillset will help you on the IT architecture journey, some of the things we are talking about are just good things to be comfortable with in day to day life. There are many occasions when you are faced with speaking to a total stranger for some reason or another. Maybe it is a silly reason like you are trying to renew a license, or maybe it is something more important like speaking to a doctor about a medical condition. If some of these things make you nervous, your public presenting and speaking skills will help make it easier. You will find that after you speak to a crowd enough times, you just do not get as nervous as you did before (though some people will always have the pre-show jitters, and there is nothing wrong with that at all).

What Could Possibly Go Wrong?

If you are not an effective presenter and verbal communicator, you may find yourself having trouble in several areas. These skills also are important when we are talking about things like gathering your customer's requirements. If you cannot effectively lead the conversation and convey the results, you will end up with a set of requirements and a design which looks nothing like what your customer is expecting.

Written Communication

This is one of the more overlooked areas of IT architecture. Sure, you can read and write, or you would not have gotten to where you are today. The question is can you communicate your thoughts and ideas using only paper? Written communication is important for an architect, as you are going to have to deliver documentation for each and every one of your engagements. Besides words to convey your story, you are also going to use things like tables and figures quite often. All these things together, which I am just going to call written communication skills, are very important for everyone, not just IT architects. Even if you decide to follow another path later, good written communication skills will always help you on your journey.

You may be hesitant to work on this area, because you are used to hearing the myth **engineers can't write**. Sure, you may be good with Visio or CAD, but when it comes to the written word, you may give up before you get started. Please do not! This is one of the greatest myths of all time, which is perpetuated by the image of someone nerdy looking with a pocket protector and taped up glasses. Those technical books you will be reading along your journey? Written by engineers. The documents you consume from a technology vendor? Written by engineers. Technical books and papers may be edited before they see the light of day, but the heavy lifting was done by the engineer who wrote it.

Later on, we will also talk about some possible career paths of an IT architect, and believe me, this skill along with your presentation skills will be handy. Presentation skills also include whiteboarding skills and diagramming skills. Remember, these soft skills are what are going to differentiate **you** as an IT architect. During the course of the journey, you are going to develop your own unique style when it comes to these skills, and it will become your calling card.

Why You Care

If your written word is the first thing a customer sees, you want it to be good. I am sure you have been on the receiving end of a lackluster proposal at some point, or even worse, a template that someone forgot to finish using the find and replace feature on. Think of how it made you feel, and make sure you never, ever pass that feeling on to your customers as an IT architect.

There are also many cases where your written word is what is going to get you a chance to show off your public presenting and speaking skills. Of course, these written skills along with those verbal skills will also take some time to hone in on. They are worth the effort, these skills will serve you well for as long as your career lasts, and then some.

Remember, as an IT architect you will be constantly delivering documentation sets to customers, both before, during, and at the end of engagement. These skills will help you put your best foot forward, and may even help you gain an edge on those you are competing with. You do realize you will have competition, right? Customers have that habit of asking for RFPs from multiple providers, not just you. I always try to go the extra mile, and ensure I am creating documentation I would be pleased with if I was on the other side of the table.

What Could Possibly Go Wrong?

U write lik dis. Rite? Y dont kustomers Like it? Do not expect to hear anything good back about the proposal you submitted. And please, just as a favor to me, do not reply to someone with the word "thx" and nothing else.

On Our Way

Now, you have received more of an introduction to the architectural building blocks. There are some of you out there who will not love all the soft skills we need to develop. If you are a highly technical individual, this is a common way to feel. One of the most fundamental transformations many IT architects make during their journeys is beginning to use these soft skills before they call on their technical skills. The more you develop and use these skills, the more you will begin to understand them, and dare I say even like them.

On the other hand, you may already have many of these soft skills, and are looking forward to refining them further during our journey. Whatever side of the path you are on right now, I hope you have a better understanding of what these skills really are, and why they are important on our journey.

Building A Server Out of Popsicle Sticks and Bubble Gum

As I am sure you already know, you will not like everything you have to do in life. It could be any number of things. Maybe the person in the cubicle next to you listens to annoying music, or you have a project which requires you to work with a technology you are not really a fan of.

You may have heard the expression, **when life gives you lemons, make lemonade**. Personally, I like to add **and sell it for a huge profit** at the end of this statement. This is good advice, and I have come up with something similar I subscribe to, as you can see by the title of this section.

When someone gives you an impossible problem, find a way to solve it. You may not be able to solve it overnight, and it may frustrate you. What is important is your thought process while solving this problem, and how you approach it. We have already talked about how there is no such thing as failure, and this is a similar approach to things.

This problem handed to you can be impossible for any number of reasons. You may not yet have the skills to solve it. You may also find the problem boring, so it is hard to get started on. You may have a very short time frame to solve this problem. Just like there is no such thing as failure, there is no such thing as impossible.

Hidden in these impossible problems are lessons, waiting for us to find them. They are not always obvious. You may have to search long and hard before you can find a lesson in a seemingly impossible problem. If there is a problem we cannot solve in the normal sense, but we learn something from working through the problem, is it still an impossible problem?

This is how I have come up with my phrase I like to use when faced with these problems. Do not panic. Use your skills to work towards a solution to the problem, and build a server out of popsicle sticks and bubble gum.

CHAPTER 7

INFRASTRUCTURE AREAS OF EXPERTISE

"An investment in knowledge pays the best interest."
— *Benjamin Franklin*

If you are thinking of classical architecture, and the design of a building, you may be very concerned with the aesthetics, and what the building is going to look like. How many windows will I have? What material will I use on the outside? How tall will it be? While designing a visually striking building may be the goal of an architect, the fact remains, there are many other things a good architect is concerned with. These other things an architect needs to account for will ultimately impact the aesthetics of the building they are designing.

The Components of an IT Architecture

Back when skyscrapers were a vision, there were some very real problems architects needed to overcome before they could build the structures of their dreams. For example, the simple problem of flushing a toilet on a higher floor. How much pressure, really would be needed to accomplish this? While an architect may not care about plumbing, plumbing requirements could alter the way they design the building. During my engineering studies at Stevens Institute of Technology, there was an eleven-story big green tower which had been built years before I arrived on campus to help determine this. Big John, as it was affectionately called, contained 44 toilets and was used to help solve this problem. This is just one example of a creative solution to a problem architects faced.

As an IT architect, you will encounter unique problems on a regular basis, and some of this creative thinking will be required of you. Your solution will undoubtedly impact numerous areas of the IT infrastructure you are designing.

Many people who have decided to undertake the IT architecture journey are an expert in one area. Perhaps that was their luck in their career so far, or it is the area they are truly passionate about. Whichever the case, you will not get very far on the journey only knowing one thing. As an IT architect, it is important to have at least a fundamental, working knowledge of each area of IT infrastructure you are going to encounter along the way. Why? Simple. Each part of the environment will depend on, impact, or talk to other areas. Take the example of a virtual machine. The virtual machine interacts with the host it runs on, the storage it runs on, and the network it connects to. This is just the virtual machine itself, not even accounting for whatever application may be running in it, which may have other dependencies.

Every IT architect has a little of this in them, after all, we are all human and we all have unique likes and dislikes. As much as you may not like a certain thing, it is important to have a well-rounded skillset to ensure you can design the bigger picture, or that your piece of the puzzle will fit into the bigger picture.

I have to admit, the application layer was not always my favorite thing to deal with, especially earlier in my career. From the get go, I was always very infrastructure oriented, I wanted to provide what those applications needed so they could run within parameters, but I did not really think beyond that. I quickly learned that I needed to have an understanding of them so I could build the infrastructure accordingly. What other servers and components did they need to talk to? Was there a database involved? What sort of network profile did they have, and was I going to need to request more space on the SAN for my ESX hosts to run them? Did they have specific performance requirements?

I am sure there are others out there with the same feeling, or perhaps you know for sure you want to be a certain type of architect, like a network architect. Maybe LAN and WAN is your passion, and you do not care about architecting anything unless it has to do with that. You are going to be in trouble quickly if you do not have an idea about what applications are running on your network, or if there is any sort of application or even storage level replication happening.

Let's take a look at some of the areas of technology an IT architect really needs to be familiar with, and more importantly, why we are concerned with them. We will also see how things can end up if we do not do our due diligence.

Infrastructure Areas of Expertise

There are many technologies in an IT infrastructure, many of which may be dependent on a specific design or specific business requirements. We are going to discuss some of the most important, and most commonly encountered infrastructure components, which are:

- Server and Compute
- Virtualization and Virtual Machines
- Network
- Storage
- Applications
- Backup and Recovery
- Business Continuity and Disaster Recovery
- Security

Sure, there are many more infrastructure and technology components out there, but this is a great starting point for any IT architect. Now, let's break down these technologies we are going to encounter along our journey.

Server and Compute

I am putting these terms together for a very important reason, some of which has to do with the next area we are going to talk about. When we talk about a server this day and age, we could mean any number of things. We may mean a physical piece of hardware in the data center, or we may mean a virtual machine. Right now, I am talking about that physical piece of hardware. Many times, it may be called a compute server, or a compute node instead of just a plain old server. You get the idea though, I am talking about the hardware with the Central Processing Units (CPUs), memory, and interface cards which is going to run some sort of workload for us. It is a good idea to understand the ins and outs of whatever server platform you are going to use in your architecture. For example, on one type of server, you may only be able to use all the PCIe slots if you have all the processor sockets filled. If you do not know something like this, it can cause issues down the road.

Why You Care

You may not be a hardware person, and that is quite alright! The fact remains, servers and compute nodes are a major part of any IT infrastructure. Servers and compute nodes are also going to interact with many other areas of an IT infrastructure. They are going to require storage, network connectivity, power and cooling, and if that was not complicated enough, there is going to be some sort of application or workload living within them. Eventually, this workload may have an issue which can be traced back to some sort of hardware problem, which is why it is important to understand how server hardware works. Now, I am going to let you in on one of the best kept secrets in the industry. If you understand how server hardware works, you can extrapolate that into almost any other sort of hardware you are going to encounter from network switches to storage arrays. At the end of the day, they all use the same concepts.

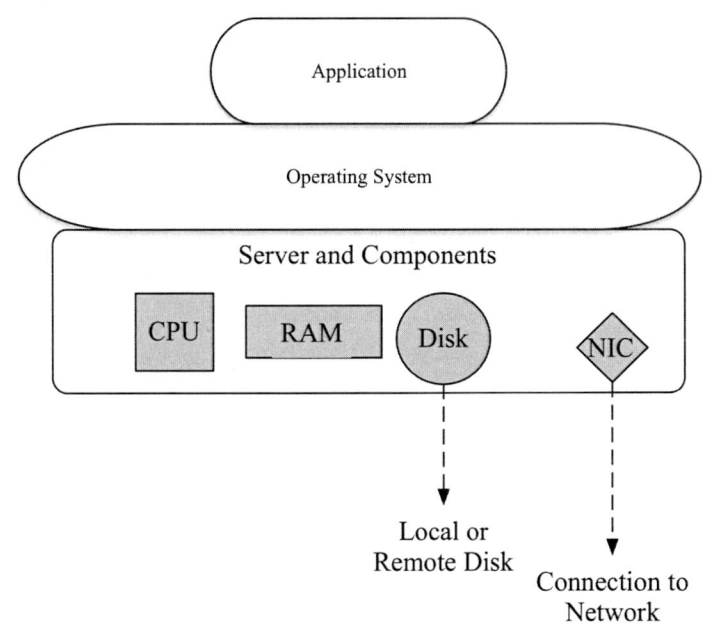

Figure 5 - Logical Diagram, Server and Compute

What Could Possibly Go Wrong?

Servers and compute nodes are something which can bring your environment to its knees quite easily any number of ways. Your application can go haywire and bring your network or storage to a screeching halt by overwhelming it, or you may have under estimated the CPU and memory requirements of your workload and are now dealing with poor performance. If you do not already understand what a server consists of, and how it works at a basic level, now is the time to learn.

Virtualization and Virtual Machines

Chances are you are going to encounter this funny little thing called virtualization in your travels. Ten years ago, it was just the cool kids, like me, paying attention to it, but now it is everywhere you look. I used to explain virtualization as running a bunch of servers on one big server. Now, depending how you architect your environment the word big is debatable, but this was a good analogy since when I started out our ESX hosts were huge in terms of CPU and memory capacity compared to the regular old servers we deployed. There are lots of ways to refer to that big server, but one of the most commonly used ones in virtualization are virtualization host, or just host. We call the little servers we run on them virtual machines or guests. There is also a name for the software which runs on the physical server and allows the guests to run on top of it. This software is called a hypervisor.

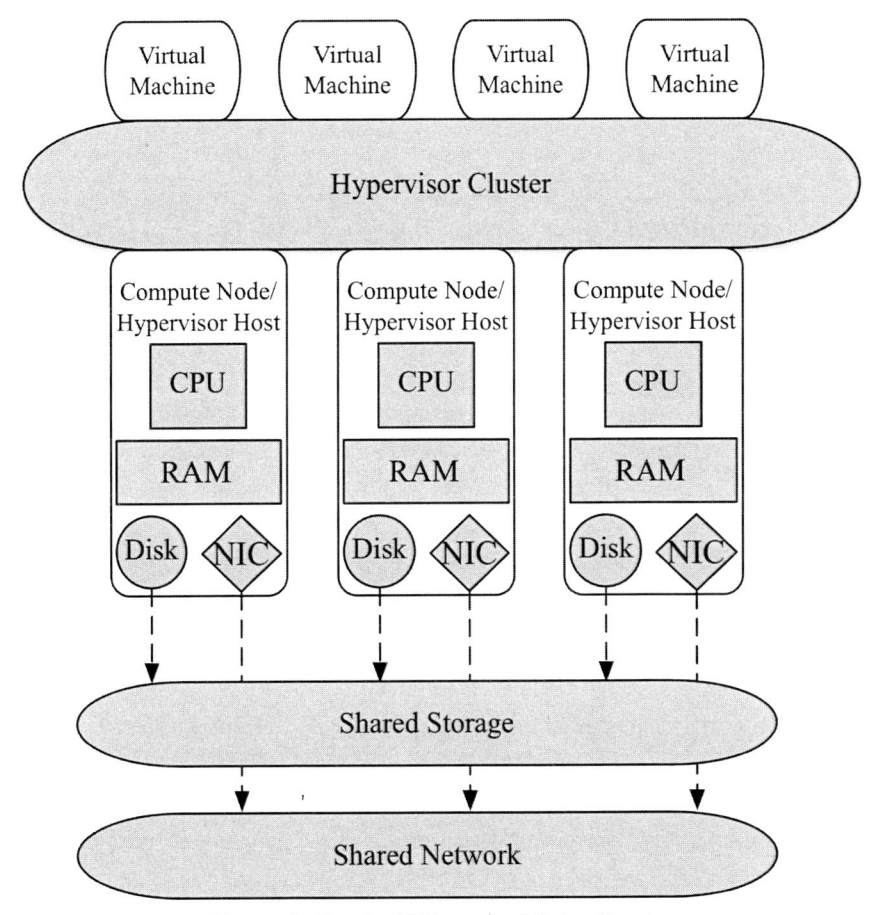

Figure 6 - Logical Diagram, Virtualization

Beyond just running lots of servers in the space, and using the same power and cooling as a big server, virtualization brings other benefits. One of the biggest ones is protection against host hardware failure. To make user of these features, hosts are placed into a group called a cluster. Virtualization software has a high availability feature which will restart the guests on surviving hosts in the cluster if the one it is running on fails. It also has load balancing software which will balance the load of the guests across the hosts. A big misconception here is that a guest can be split up and run on multiple hosts, which is not the case. VMware vSphere however does have a feature called VMware Fault Tolerance which runs copies of the same virtual machine on multiple hosts. This way, if the host the virtual machine is running on fails, it continues running without interruption instead of having to restart on a surviving host.

There are many more features and benefits to virtualization, which vary depending on which software suite you are using as your hypervisor, and hypervisor management. Picking the correct hypervisor can be a critical part of any IT architecture. Of course, I feel the need to add the disclaimer that I am a huge fan of VMware, if you had not already figured it out. Nonetheless, we will talk about how to get exposure to all sorts of hypervisors later on.

Now, when we talk about virtualization, we may be talking about virtualizing more than just servers, but that is another topic we will address soon, do not worry.

Why You Care

Virtualization is everywhere, so it is important to have a good understanding of how it works. Remember what our servers and compute nodes needed? CPU, memory, network connectivity and storage? Virtual machines need these same resources, so now you are dealing with two layers of networking and storage at the very least, and making sure you have enough CPU and Memory resources since they are being shared among many virtual machines.

IT Architect Series: The Journey

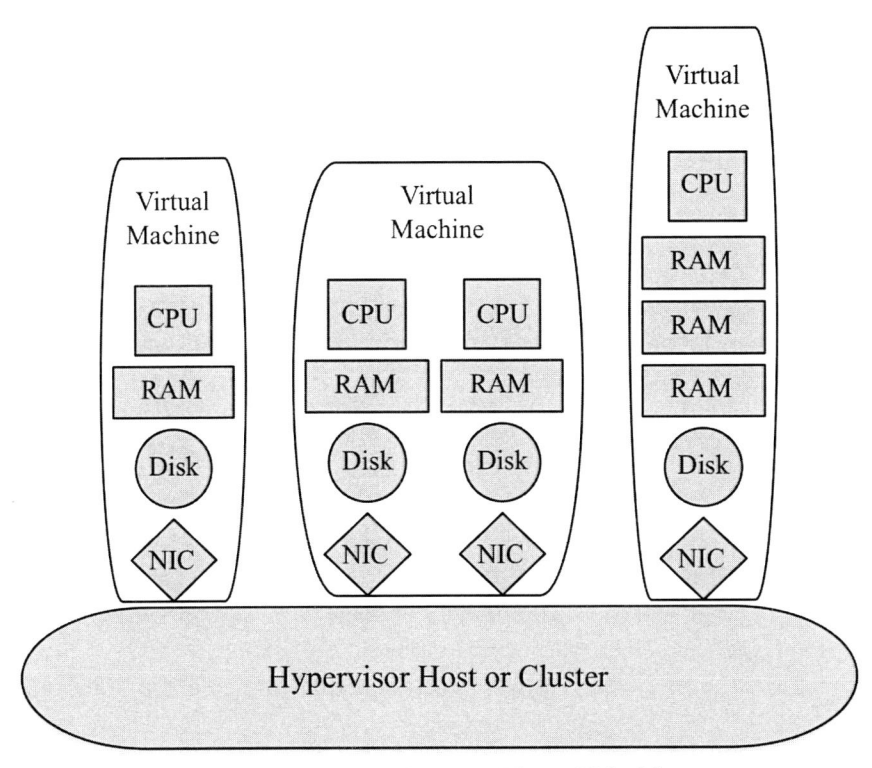

Figure 7 - Logical Diagram, Virtual Machines

The best part about virtual machines is you can configure as many or as few resources as you need to meet your requirements. You can also change these later if required.

After you pick the hypervisor that meets your customer's requirements, there is still much design work to be done at the hypervisor level. You are going to need to understand how it interacts with the supporting components in your infrastructure, and even beyond that depending on what type of applications will be hosted on it.

What Could Possibly Go Wrong?

That one server that went haywire before? You can take all the problems you could possibly have with a server and multiply them when you enter the realm of virtualization. There is also a new area for wrongdoers to attack, and that is your hypervisor environment. It quickly becomes a mission critical portion of the infrastructure when it is in use, and like anything else, it is vulnerable to attack.

Network

You are going to have to deal with the network in some way, shape, or form. The network is the backbone of any infrastructure, especially with the rise of converged and hyperconverged infrastructure today. The network has been around since the dawn of IT architecture, and if you are really lucky, you will encounter a network from that time period. While that last line was sort of sarcastic it is generally true. It is not uncommon to encounter a network designed over 20 years ago, even if it is using currently supported hardware.

Networking is one of the more complex topics when it comes to infrastructure, because there are so many ways a network can be implemented. When we are talking about our LAN, and where things are happening, we are often talking about Layer 2, or switching. That does not mean you do not have to have an understanding of Layer 3, or routing as well. It will depend on your specific environment and workload, but if you really want to get confused, now there are networking devices that operate at both Layer 2 and Layer 3.

IT Architect Series: The Journey

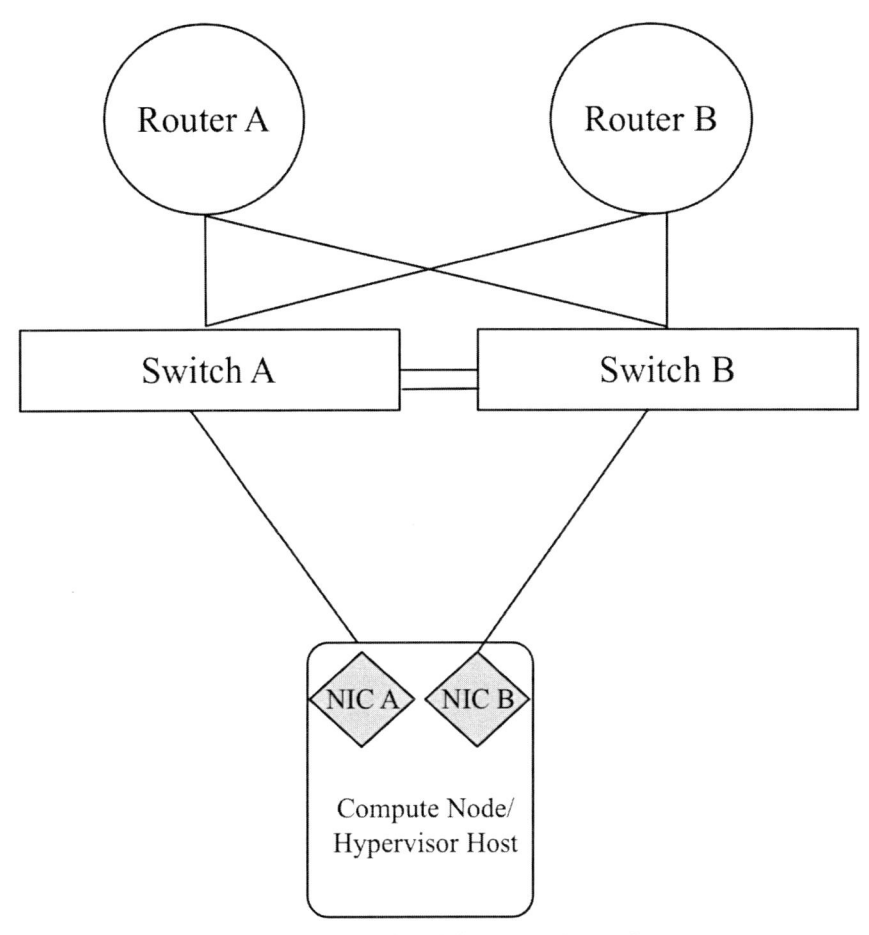

Figure 8 - Logical Diagram, Network

Speaking of the unique environment you are interacting with, we also need to be concerned with what area of the network we are working with. Are we only concerned with LAN traffic? What about WAN traffic? How do the customer's various sites communicate with each other? How is remote access provided? These are all things we need to consider when we are architecting any infrastructure solution.

Now that you understand some of the ways a network may be implemented, get ready to throw all of what you already know out the window. In recent years, a new type of networking has materialized. Welcome to network virtualization. This is a topic worth exploring after you have learned more about the fundamentals of traditional networking during your journey.

Why You Care

I have met many who are almost afraid of the network, but it is time to face the facts. You are going to impact the network somehow, and it will also impact you and your design choices. Think you can get away from the network by building a career in application architecture since that is not a **real** infrastructure component anyway? Sorry. That application is going to talk to the other infrastructure components it relies on somehow, and that somehow is using the network.

Let's not forget about converged networking either. You may be running both your standard Ethernet traffic as well as your storage traffic over the same fiber, and through the same devices. IP based storage protocols such as iSCSI and NFS are exceedingly popular since they do not require a dedicated SAN switching infrastructure. The same can be said about Fibre Channel over Ethernet or FCoE, as long as the network equipment you are using supports it.

I am going to skip ahead a little bit and teach you something about storage. What if you need to use a dedicated Fibre Channel infrastructure? While it does have some uniqueness, the general concepts of networking apply here, except the devices, connections, and frames are different. A solid understanding of networking will only help you when you go down the storage path.

Also see Network Virtualization above. You are going to encounter it in some way, shape, or form soon, I promise.

What Could Possibly Go Wrong?

If you are not aware of the load your infrastructure could put on the existing network, or you are not taking it into account when designing a new network, you are going to run into trouble for sure. You configured QoS (Quality of Service) correctly to get around what happens when that other architect did not do their network homework, right?

Storage

Storage is one of those critical parts of an infrastructure which is often underestimated and overlooked, especially in the world of virtualization. All those virtual machines? They are going to consume storage in any number of ways, so you must be ready for them. When it boils down to it, everything is going to consume storage one way or another, it is just a matter of where the consumption happens.

One of the most common places this storage will reside on is a storage array. A storage array is nothing more than a fancy, high powered server with many, many disks attached to it. Your storage array is going to connect to your infrastructure somehow, and you guessed it, it is going to need a network. In some cases, based on the storage protocol you use, you may take advantage of the IP-based network you currently have or are architecting. Perhaps you will take advantage of a dedicated IP network just for storage, which is not the same as a Storage Area Network or SAN. While a SAN will be a dedicated network for storage, it functions slightly differently than an IP network, although the general concepts are the same.

We also mentioned storage protocols, which there are numerous choices such as Fiber Channel, FCoE, iSCSI, Network File Service (NFS), Server Message (SMB) or its derivative Common Interface File Service (CIFS). As an IT architect, it is going to be up to you to pick the right combination of storage protocols, storage hardware, and storage software. Oh, and do not forget to make sure your physical storage is using the correct disks too, or you are in for a nasty surprise.

These days, an easy way to get around having to worry about the performance of your disks is to use Solid State Drives, or SSDs. While they are one of the fastest things in town, they also come with a price tag associated with it. Yes, the prices of SSDs are falling every day, but we are not at the point where we can use them for everything and still be cost effective. Your budget can have a huge impact on your storage environment, and it is up to you, as the architect, to figure out what is best for your customer.

Melissa Palmer

The other types of drives are SATA and SAS drives, which of course both have their benefits and trade-offs. SAS drives can provide more input/output operations per second, more commonly known as IOPS. This, of course is a simplification of things, but it is a good starting place that most people may not have if they have not been involved with storage. We will talk more about the different disk types later. I used to be one of those people, and I thought Fibre Channel was one of the most confusing things ever when I started to dive deeper, since it was both a disk type and a protocol (this may be one of the reasons I am not the biggest fan of Fibre Channel, but I digress).

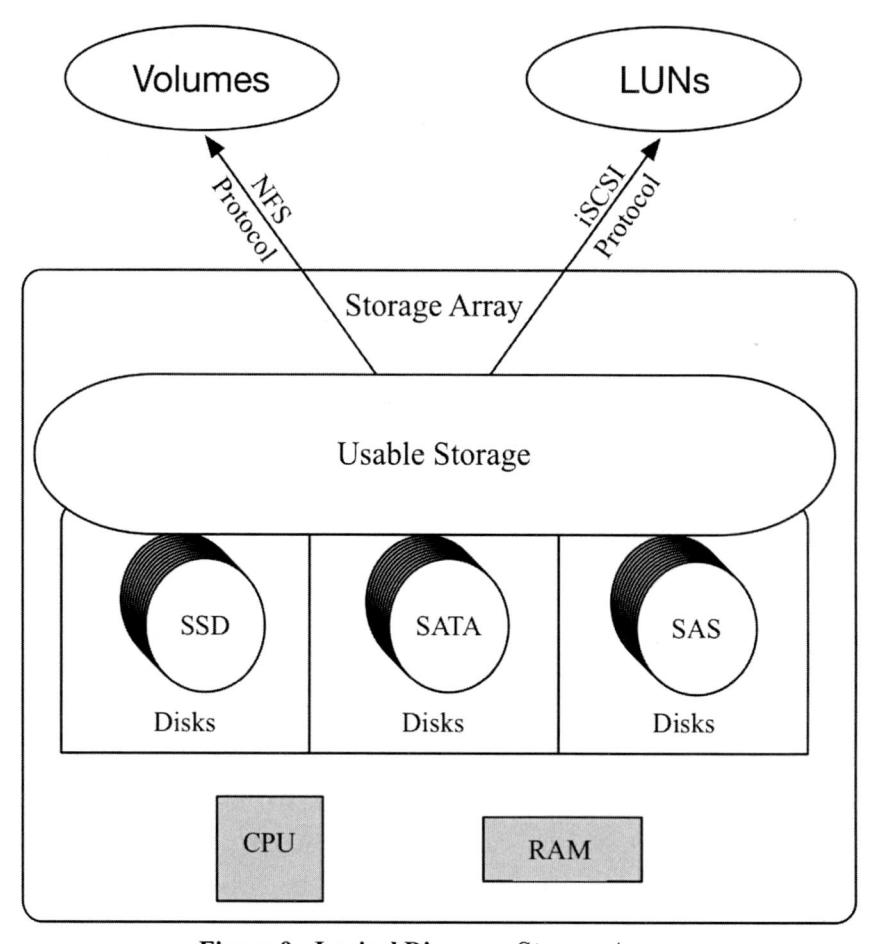

Figure 9 - Logical Diagram, Storage Array

Why You Care

Storage is going to be become an even more critical piece of your infrastructure if you are virtualizing the environment. Your virtual machines all have virtual hard disks, which need to be stored on a physical disk someplace. You are also going to have to make sure these disks have ample performance and connectivity to serve your environment. A SSD array would be rather useless if it only had two 1-Gbps Ethernet connections in the back of it, wouldn't it?

What Could Possibly Go Wrong

A well architected storage solution will run like a dream, but if there are issues it can quickly become a nightmare. For example, if you are going to try to run your production virtual machines on 6 TB SATA drives with no cache, there is a good chance you are about to learn a lot about suffering. The disks simply will not be able to keep up with your virtual machines, especially during boot storms or other periods of high I/O.

Applications

So, finally, after everything is said and done, you have built this fantastic IT infrastructure. Well, at least you think you did. The fact of the matter is you have not unless you can ensure the applications you need to run in the environment perform as needed, giving special care to an organization's mission critical applications.

What is a mission critical application, anyway, you ask? Many times, they may also be called business critical applications. We answer this question with our classic answer to every architecture question which comes our way: **it depends**. Each organization will use different application classifications, and the criticality of the applications will depend on a number of things, for example, how the company actually makes money, and the company's main business objectives are.

Just because you are designing an infrastructure does not mean you are necessarily supporting mission critical applications. You may be designing a sandbox environment, or a shared infrastructure for other applications. On the other hand, you may be putting in an environment for the company's number one business application. These two situations would, of course, be architected differently. This is why understanding your customer's requirements is so very important.

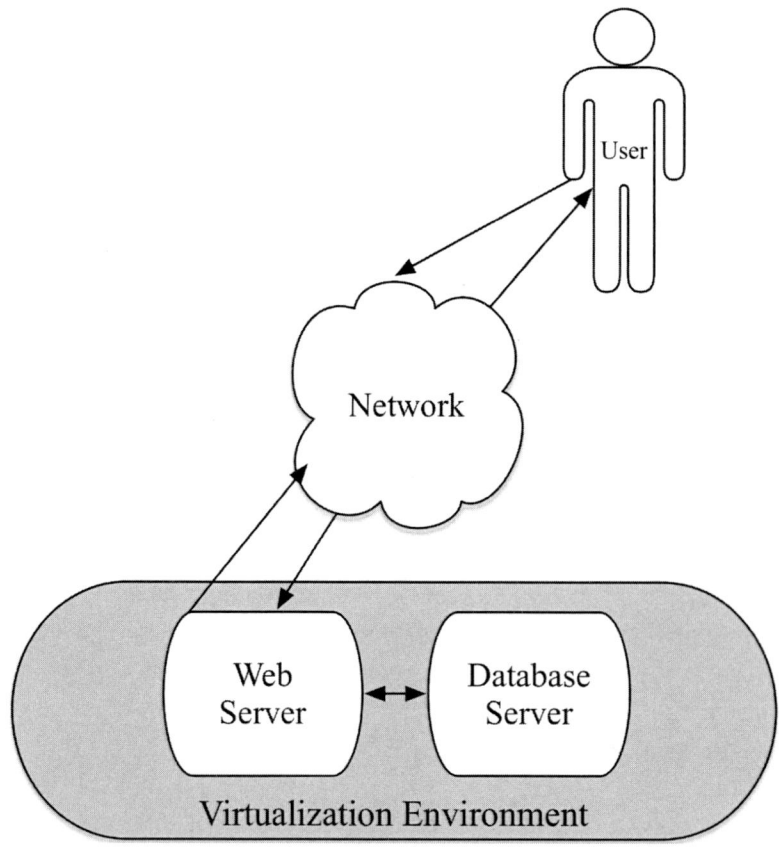

Figure 10 - Logical Diagram, Web Application

Why You Care

If you are looking to be an IT architect, applications are the reason you even have a job. If you are truly going to provide a solution which meets your customer's requirements, you are going to have to know how their applications work. I am not saying you need to be an expert on every little application out there, but you should have an understanding on how different applications work (such as an application with a web front end and a backend database), and how their supporting components like databases and webservers work. The knowledge you gain about learning new things during your IT architecture journey will almost always come into play when it is time to talk about a customer's applications. You may find similarities with other applications you have previously encountered, or you will be using your skills to learn this new application, especially when the applications are developed in-house.

What Could Possibly Go Wrong

The short answer? Well, everything. If your infrastructure cannot run the required applications, you are in big, big trouble. Applications are not to be overlooked, they are the reason IT infrastructure exists in the first place.

Backup and Recovery

While it is a great accomplishment to launch an IT infrastructure, and the associated applications it is designed for, that does not mean much if you cannot recover it when something goes wrong. It is very important to make sure you have backed up the various components of your infrastructure such as the configuration of hardware components, software components, and the applications themselves. Beyond just backing things up, you need to be able to recover them and meet your RTO. Backups do not mean anything if you cannot recover from them.

There is not necessarily one backup and recovery tool or method to rule them all. As an IT architect, you are going to make sure you can account for the successful backup and recovery of each and every component you implement. You may be able to do this by simply exporting a configuration for backup, and re-importing it for recovery. Other components will give you more trouble. It will all depend on the hardware and software you have used in your design.

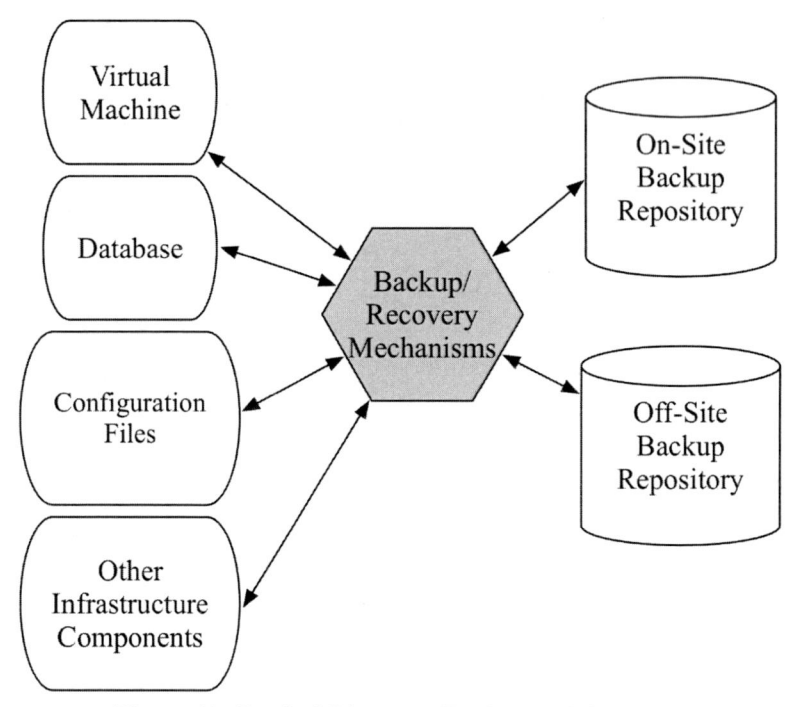

Figure 11 - Logical Diagram, Backup and Recovery

Why You Care

You are going to have backup and recovery tests as part of the validation of the solution you have architected. It is much easier to plan for this as you are designing things, than to scramble at the last second trying to figure out how you are going to backup and restore everything. The business you are providing a solution for is going to have to meet their RTOs and RPOs with the solution you have designed from them. As we mentioned before, these RTOs and RPOs need to align with the customer's SLAs. If they do not, it should be big red flag to you, and you are going to have to work with them to perform a Business Impact Analysis (BIA) to ensure the solution will truly support their business requirements.

Beyond just checking the box to make sure you can back up and restore everything, you are going to have to make sure the customer is able to carry these tasks out. This is why so many organizations have the almost always dreaded backup and recovery tests. These are important skills to practice for everyone involved, since stress and nerves will be running hot in the event of an actual disaster.

What Could Possibly Go Wrong

I have seen many IT architects focus on backup times, backup speeds, and all those great things, but not be concerned about the same for recovery. The worst that can possibly happen is you cannot recover an environment at all, essentially crippling and destroying a business. Does that scare you? It should. You may also not be able to meet an organizations RPOs and RTOs and violate their SLA, costing them money, or again, putting them out of business. You get my point, right? If you leave this part out, you really have not delivered anything useful at all.

Business Continuity and Disaster Recovery

Business Continuity and Disaster Recovery tie heavily into backup and recovery. The tools you use to backup and recover your environment are often the tools you will use in the event of a disaster.

If your background at this point is purely technical, this may be one of the most difficult concepts to grasp. There are multiple components to meeting the challenges Business Continuity and Disaster Recovery bring. One component we have are the business drivers behind them such as our RPOs, RTOs, and SLAs, which we will discuss in more detail soon. We also have the tools and technologies we are going to use to meet them.

When we talked about backup and recovery, we touched a little bit on disaster recovery tests. Since some of the tools you may use are the same for recovering from a mistake and recovering from a disaster, I am going to mention them again. A term you will hear a lot about is **runbooks**. Runbooks are basically the scripts those preforming the recovery process are going to use in the event of a disaster. There are two types of runbooks: automated runbooks and manual runbooks. Both are hotly debated, and the type you choose to use will depend on you guessed it, your customer's business requirements.

Automation is of course the panacea for technology problems at the moment. Everyone wants to automate everything in sight, and automating the failover of an environment or application certainly has its benefits. Some organizations, however are not comfortable with total automation, so you may be using a combination of automated and manual runbooks.

The process to failover may be automated via workflows and scripts, but many customers still want some sort of human intervention before the failover takes place. For example, an operator may be instructed to perform several tests and call the Site B NOC before they press the **play** button on a recovery work flow. On the flip side, some customers may want to architect everything so seamlessly, where they do not even care if there is a failover since the application is designed to run at full capacity in another site.

The bottom line is at the end of the day, the business needs to be able to run in the event of a disaster. The **how** is up to you, as the IT architect.

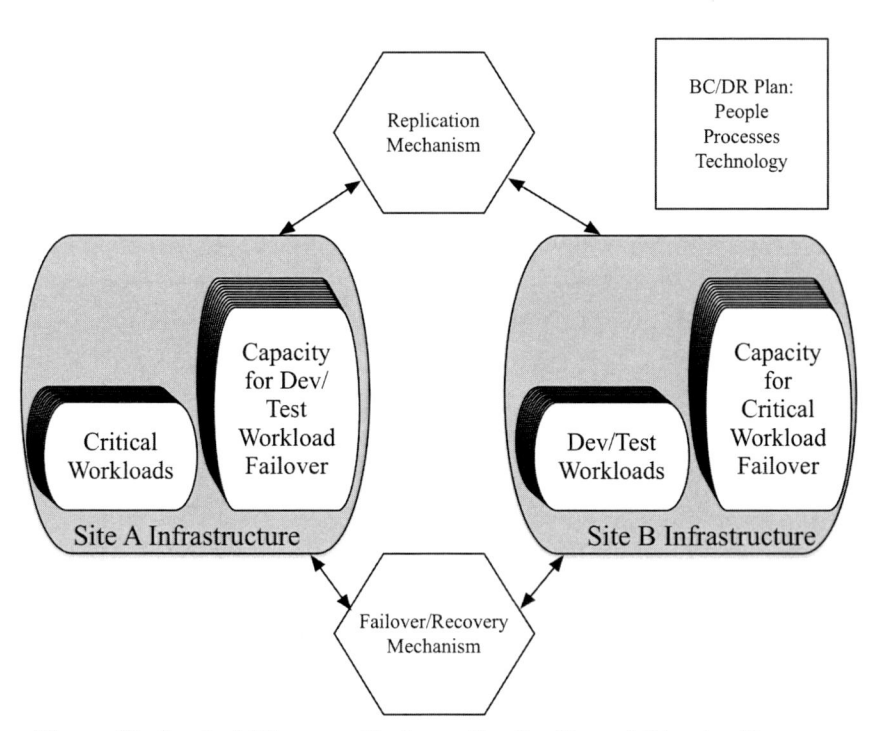

Figure 12 - Logical Diagram, Business Continuity and Disaster Recovery

Why You Care

You may be sick of reading RPO, RTO, and SLA by now, and wonder why I insist on beating this dead horse over and over again. That is because these concepts are important. Remember, we are here as architects to solve business problems, and one of the biggest business problems a customer can have is when their business stops running for whatever reason.

It up to you to flesh all of this out with your customer. You are also going to need to either update existing runbooks, or create new ones, whether they be manual or automated, as part of the IT architecture engagement.

Something you will also need to account for is the human factor. If the last ten disaster recovery tests have been successful for a customer, do you really want to come in and change everything in one fell swoop? Perhaps the better solution would be to gradually introduce new runbooks over time, ensuring the prior, successful runbooks are still able to be used in the event of a disaster.

What Could Possibly Go Wrong

The zombies ate one of my data centers, then they broke into my second surviving data center and ate my manual runbook. The company no longer exists. Sure, this may sound extreme, but these are serious topics we are talking about. Disasters happen, whether they be natural or man-made. If an organization has not done business continuity and disaster recovery planning, they are going to be in big trouble at some point. It is not **if** a disaster hits, it is **when** a disaster hits.

Security

Security is a very broad topic, and will have different meanings in every area of IT infrastructure. In short, security is about making sure the correct people have the correct access to the correct things. It is about making sure someone cannot gain access to a system or environment that should not be there in the first place. You will also hear a lot about vulnerabilities, which are when software has something unexpected in it which can enable an attacker to gain access to someplace they should not be. Security is also about managing both internal and external access to systems.

Internally, it is about making sure people are not doing things like leaving their password on a sticky note on their monitor, and are not sharing their login information with others. It is also about making sure a single account does not have the keys to the kingdom. The goal is to make sure the users can carry out their job functions, and nothing else. You may not want your storage team to have access to your network switches unless there is a real business need for them to do so.

Externally, it is about not letting the attackers in. This is no easy feat, and it takes a sophisticated set of tools like intrusion detection systems (IDSs) and intrusion protection systems (IPSs). It is also about doing simple things like making sure the passwords on the edge routers are not left at the default values. The list of things organizations do to protect themselves goes on and on and on.

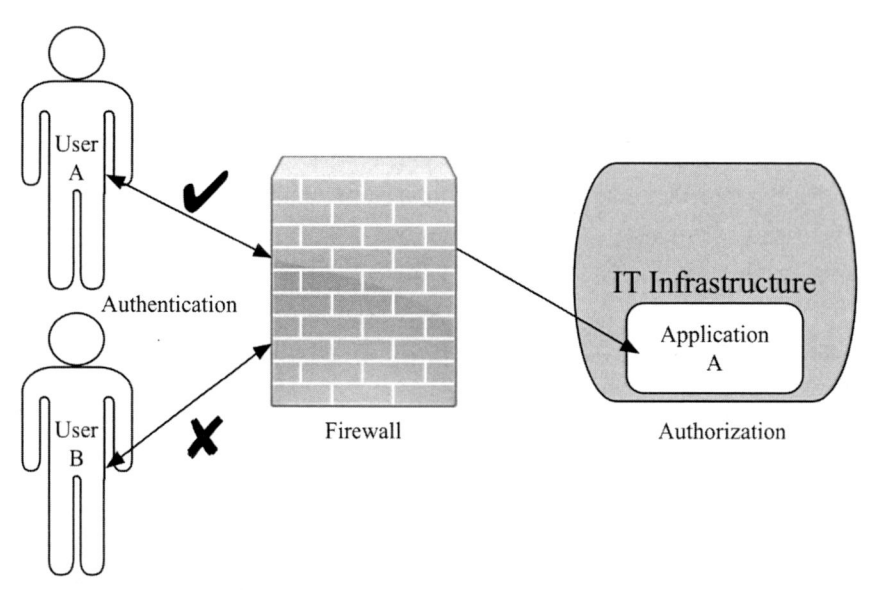

Figure 13 - Logical Diagram, Security

Why You Care

If there is one area of infrastructure I do not have to talk you into learning about, it is security. Chances are, you have been the victim of some sort of data breach at one point or another. It could have been something like a retailer you shopped with, or a website you had a login for. These costs organizations millions and millions of dollars, and the more sensitive the information, the more it costs. If you have been the unfortunate victim of having your very personal information stolen from a company you trusted, they have most likely provided you with some sort of identity management service, which does not come cheap.

Security is a big part of any IT architecture you create. As an IT architect, it is important to make sure you are creating an environment with security in mind. You should be consulting with the security organization at your customer, and making sure you are in line with their recommendations and processes. The earlier you engage them the better. If you do not, you may be inadvertently non-compliant with organization's security policy, which will cause trouble later. You also may find yourself in a situation where an organization does not have a very strong mindset when it comes to security. In this case, it is your job to use your expertise to try to enhance the security of what you are designing.

During the requirements gathering phase of your project, you should be able to get a good handle on how important security is to your customer, and how you can support their security programs. Security can also negatively impact manageability at times, so it is important to keep your customer's requirements in mind. While we want to say, there is no such thing as a solution too secure, the fact remains there is only so much some administrators are willing to put up with in the name of security. Part of your job is striking this balance.

What Could Possibly Go Wrong

If you turn on the news one morning and see that your customer was hacked, and the data appears to be from the system you architected, that will not be a good thing. At all. For anyone involved. I am sure you have seen many unfortunate examples in the news lately, just imagine if you were the person responsible for any of them.

Other Technologies

The technologies we are going to talk about as part of your journey are more than enough to get you started on the road to becoming an IT architect. At some point, you are going to encounter some sort of technology we have not discussed here. I cannot tell you when it will be, and I cannot tell you what it will be. I can tell you, however, one of my biggest goals by the time we are done is to make sure you have the skills you need to immerse yourself in that new technology and learn it. Reading this book alone will not make you an IT architect, but it will be your guide along the journey. Even after we are done here, the journey will continue, and you will have the tools you need to make the next trek.

Let's take a look at some of the hottest up and coming technologies, and why the core infrastructure areas of expertise still matter along with them.

Graphics Processing Units and Machine Learning

For a long time, I know when I thought of a Graphics Processing Unit, or GPU, I thought of, well video games, and the beautiful 3D rendering accompanying them when you had a good GPU in your computer. Today, GPUs are used for a lot more than just gaming. While both CPUs and GPUs contain processors, the similarities stop there.

GPUs have many more cores than CPUs, which make them an ideal candidate for processing parallel tasks. You can scale GPUs to thousands of cores, while CPUs cores are measured in tens. GPU also consume less power, and you can get many more of them in a powerful server than you can CPUs.

Because of the way GPUs can process, they are often used in machine learning and deep learning applications. Think of machine learning as algorithms which can evolve as they process more and more data, and can also receive massive amounts of data, like live audio or video as their input sources. One of the most popular applications of machine learning right now is self-driving cars. This gives you an idea of the massive amount of data machine learning systems are capable of processing.

Why the Infrastructure Areas of Expertise Still Matter

GPUs still rely heavily on the other infrastructure areas of expertise. While these applications are not relying on the CPU for all their computations, the underlying server still must have network and storage connections, which often need to be high speed to be able to store all the data the machine learning application is processing. Think of GPUs as an addition to a compute server. Now, virtual machines can even be configured to access the GPUs on a hypervisor host. Over the next several years, we are going to hear more and more about the addition of GPUs to infrastructure environments.

Hyperconverged Infrastructure

Hyperconverged Infrastructure, which you may also see referred to as HCI, seeks to make infrastructure easier to manage and consume. To do this, the storage and compute environments are combined into a single node which performs both functions. Then, when you need capacity on either side, you add additional nodes for the system. This model also provides high availability functionality for both the compute and storage platforms, you will need to implement at least several nodes to get started.

Why the Infrastructure Areas of Expertise Still Matter

Hyperconverged infrastructure is often spun as a magical box. One thing often overlooked here is the network aspect, which hyperconverged infrastructures rely heavily on. Sure, you are combining compute and storage, but the rest of the stack you are dealing with is what we are already accustomed to. The magic in HCI comes in its ease of use and scalability, and the ability for any complexities to be hidden or solved by well-designed software. When looking at HCI as an infrastructure solution, always make sure it meets your customer's business requirements. Just like any other technology, sometimes it will be a fit, and other times it will not.

Cloud

Cloud is another one of those things seen as magical. When the cloud first began catching on, customers were wooed with the ability to burst into the cloud as they saw fit. After all, it would be so much cheaper and easier than building things in house, right? That did not quite work out to be the case, but there are many other circumstances where cloud can be a good fit for a business.

Why the Infrastructure Areas of Expertise Still Matter

At the end of the day, the cloud is nothing more than someone else's data center. Because it is someone else's data center, it still has all the components we are familiar with. As an IT architect, we are still responsible for designing an infrastructure as we would if the solution were on premises, but now we must use the tools and technologies we are given in the cloud.

Many cloud companies perform a twist on the components we are used to, and use their own compute and storage products, which of course, are simply made up of commodity hardware running well-designed software. Software-defined networking also comes into play in these massively scalable environments. Have we noticed a trend here?

The trend is something I like to call SDE or Software Defined Everything. These days, the hardware we can purchase off the shelf is just so fast, it does not matter as much as it used to. It just does not make much sense for innovation budgets to be spent developing custom hardware any longer. The benefit to those who sell hardware and software together is the ability to ensure the software runs flawlessly on a specific hardware configuration, and to limit the ability for someone who purchases their product to change and break things. This is also why you will see hardware compatibility lists for software solutions, to ensure the components have been tested to work together.

Containers

If you thought virtual machines were amazing, just wait until you start playing with containers. Containers are a light weight, well, container, which simply holds the software which needs to run. We no longer need to deploy a dedicated operating system to run each application. The container has the ability to leverage the what it needs from the operating system of the host it is running on. This results in less overhead, and more portability. I can move this container to almost anywhere in my infrastructure, since we have added another level of abstraction. The container my developer is creating on their laptop can easily be moved to the data center and into production.

Why the Infrastructure Building Blocks Still Matter

By this point, I am sure you already know what I am going to say. The host the containers run on? You guessed it, they still have CPU, memory, network, and storage resources attached to them. When containerizing an application, building resiliency and high availability into the application itself is key. We do not care about containers the way we cared about virtual machines. In most cases, the containers themselves are not even backed up. If a container or host dies, a new container is simply spun up on a new host. What we do need to worry about is backing up any persistent storage the container has attached to it, as well as any databases it connects to. We just care about our application data, not about the container housing the application itself.

This is vastly different than the way many use virtual machines. Virtual machines need a lot of care and maintenance, after all, we need to worry about keeping them up to date with patches. With containers and a distributed application, you can just replace the containers with new ones, instead of going through the effort of updating them. While the effort of updating a virtual machine itself has been simplified over the years, the real effort still comes in the coordination of outage and maintenance windows. By changing the way applications are architected, this can be mostly eliminated, although of course, the new version of the container should still be tested before it is rolled into production.

On Our Way

Next up on our journey, we are going to get out our walking stick and start to conquer those mountains we see in the distance. We are going to go through each of the infrastructure areas of expertise one by one, and I am going to give you some tips, tricks, and advice for increasing your skills in these areas. You will be able to use these methods to learn about technologies you encounter in the future.

My advice to you, as an aspiring IT architect is to make sure you have still got some time carved out during your journey to keep an eye on what is happening in the infrastructure world. I know I have been tempted to dive in 100% and focus solely on the journey at times, but doing this can be a real disservice to yourself. For example, I defended my VCDX design on VMware vSphere 5.5. A big part of me wanted to spend 100% of my time on VMware vSphere 5.5, but the fact was VMware vSphere 6.0 was already out, and VMware vSphere 6.5 came out only weeks before my defense.

Even though I needed to use VMware vSphere 5.5 due to my customer's requirements, I would be doing them a disservice if I was not familiar with the new features in changes in later VMware vSphere versions. Why? So I could ensure I was designing an environment with the future in mind. Things change between software versions, and new technologies are always emerging. A big part of our jobs as architects is evaluating how these emerging technologies could impact our infrastructures in the future.

As you can see, being willing and able to pick up new and emerging technologies is required of any good IT architect. This way, when you come across something beyond what we are going to spend our time on here, you will be ready. We are going to be focusing on the infrastructure areas of expertise we have defined here. While focusing on these, you will be gaining new tools to add to your learning arsenal along the journey. You will be able to apply these tools and lessons to almost everything you encounter in the future.

CHAPTER 8

CONNECTING THE INFRASTRUCTURE AREAS OF EXPERTISE

"Humans are allergic to change. They love to say, 'We've always done it this way.' I try to fight that. That's why I have a clock on my wall that runs counter-clockwise."
— Grace Hopper

Following our analogy of constructing a building, the infrastructure areas of expertise are things like electricity, plumbing, and the actual structure of the building. If you leave out any of these areas, you simply do not have a building at all. By combining these infrastructure areas of expertise along with the architectural building blocks, at the end of the project you will have created a building with the exact features your client was looking for. The building will be tall and glimmering in the sunlight, and the inside will be perfectly suited to meet their needs. Your client will feel like they have always belonged here.

Building Your Foundation

Now, we are going to look at the foundational technical skills of an IT architect. I am going to use my experience, and what I learned along my journey to help guide you in enhancing your skills in each of these areas. The foundation of a data center is just like the foundation of a house or building. If you do not build a solid foundation, it does not matter what you build on top. You could build the most amazing, tall, gorgeous structure, but if the foundation is not solid, it can collapse. If you plan the foundation correctly, this building will be around for generations to come.

IT architects look at a data center the same way. If the foundation of the infrastructure within the data center is not strong, there will be problems down the road. The environment may not be able to scale, or it may not even be able to handle the capacity initially needed if it was not designed correctly. There are also the more physical aspects to think about in the data center. If you do not plan for your customer's projected growth, you could quickly run out of cooling capacity before you run out of network capacity.

No matter what is being designed and built, the foundation is the most crucial aspect.

A Word on Specific Vendors

I am going to do the best I can to keep things vendor agnostic. When it comes down to it, everyone has their favorite vendors to work with, usually because they have had good experiences with that specific piece of technology. As IT architects, we are tied to our customer's business driven requirements, which means we do not always get to work with the vendors and technologies we are most familiar with and like the best. You will, however, find that if you learn a specific vendor's product, you will also learn how underlying technology works as well.

During the journey, when we are trying to gain experience, usually we will take whatever comes our way. If you end up developing a skillset with a certain vendor because that is what your company uses, do not worry about it now right now. Learn what you can. Remember, a new technology is easy to pick up, once you understand the theory behind it. This same theory also applies to learning a new language. Once you determine the best way for you to learn this language, the next language is much easier to learn.

Beginning Your Journey

Before you start getting your hands dirty packing for the journey, you should have a heart to heart talk with your manager wherever you work right now. This is for a couple of reasons. First, there is a good chance you can work things to benefit your job now, as well as your career. When you write your yearly goals for your job, chances are there is a section for personal development. It would not hurt to put some of the things you are going to work on during your IT architecture journey here. This applies to both soft skills and technology skills. By doing this, we just made part of your journey your job, so hopefully you can get paid for it. Make sure to clearly understand how much time your manager thinks is reasonable to work on developing these skills.

A good manager should encourage you to develop all your skills, not just the ones related to the job you are doing right now. We will talk how to deal with an unsupportive manager in a bit, but I am hoping you do not encounter this hurdle.

You should also ask your manager about seeking out old hardware. You are going to need some servers and some switches to get started. A storage array would be nice, but you can get away with storage internal to your servers when you are getting started. This is also a great opportunity to dig into some areas you may not be familiar with. Think about determining the power requirements of this old equipment, and how much it will cost to run it. It is also a great way to practice some of you diagramming skills, by creating several diagrams for your proposed lab. Rack elevation diagrams and connectivity diagrams are a good starting point.

After you get the go or no go from your manager, listen closely to what refresh projects are going on. When you find out hardware is destined for the big data center in the sky, ask whoever owns the old equipment if they would be willing to spare some for you to build a lab. This should work out one of three ways for you. First, you will get the equipment and be able to build yourself a lab. Second, you will find out the equipment is destined for that team's lab, and you will be able to get access to it. Third, you will just hear no, which we can also deal with.

You should also find out what teams do in fact have labs, and if they are willing to give you access. Do not just walk up to a stranger and ask for lab access. First, you should become friendly with whoever's lab you are going to want to ask for access to, this will help you with more than just some equipment access in the future.

When Your Manager is a Mangler

The nicest term I can come up with when you have a not so great manager is a mangler. I, along with others, coined this term when we were working with a product with the word "manager" in the name many years ago. This can apply to a manager as well, as one who mangles. Your direct manager may not be a mangler, but if you have a mangler in your management chain, you are going to have a bad time. You have more than likely already figured out if you are dealing with one of these.

Unfortunately, the only way to get away from one of these is to get out of the situation. You can do this a couple of ways. First, you can try to transfer to a different team within the same company, or leave and go to a different company. Each of these methods have pros and cons, which I will leave up to you to determine based on your requirements. If you are not happy in your current place of employment, and you have the ability to attempt a change, I encourage you to do so. We spend so much of our time at work; it really is a shame to not be happy during this time. I am not talking about a project or person you do not like here and there, since we are all bound to deal with these at one time or another. I am talking the deep-seated misery that is being unhappy in your job. If this is the case for you, I hope you can find a better place to work as part of your journey to becoming an IT architect.

You do not necessarily have to have a supportive manager to become an IT architect, but if you have a manager who is willing to let you work with other teams cross-functionally, it will certainly give you more opportunities for learning at work.

Making the Most Out of What You Have Now

I have a couple more tips for you to get the most out of your current role. Of course, they do require extra work and sometimes longer hours. If you are in a supportive environment, these things can work in your favor. If not, do not worry, I have some other ideas for getting experience.

The first thing you should do is to volunteer to be on call for any sort of maintenance which requires someone from your team to be involved. When I was a virtualization administrator, and I had a funny feeling I was heading to do something with storage next. I volunteered to be on call for storage maintenance. Technically I just had to stay online long enough to babysit my VMware ESX hosts, but I stayed on the line and observed the storage maintenance. This gave me a good idea of what kinds of things the storage administrators had to do (software updates and configuration changes for one), and the things they were concerned about. I also made a list of things they were talking about that I did not understand for me to research later. This was a great opportunity, but required me sacrificing some Friday nights. This tactic works well, so keep it in mind as we discuss the infrastructure areas of expertise.

The Infrastructure Areas of Expertise

Before we dive into the specific infrastructure areas we are going to be working on during our journey, let's take a moment to review what they are:

- Server and Compute
- Virtualization and Virtual Machines
- Network
- Storage
- Applications
- Backup and Recovery
- Business Continuity and Disaster Recovery
- Security

I hope you get so sick and tired of seeing these lists of skills, that you know them off the top of your head. After all, you never know where an IT architecture conversation will go after you have started it. You may start with a discussion of network architecture, and be asked about how the network relates to the rest of the infrastructure. At that point, you should have a good understanding of what infrastructure pieces you are going to need to put together to solve the problems of your customers.

As we move on to the different infrastructure areas of expertise, and how to gain experience with them, there is going to be a lot of information. If I mention something like a specific resource I have found helpful, or a general method which helped me, I will also include it in the Resources Appendix. This way these resources are in a single, handy place for you to refer to as you continue your journey. Remember, this is just a starting place for you. Soon you will be discovering new resources, and applying the learning methods we have talked about. You may even discover more learning methods that really resonate with you. Remember, there is all the information and knowledge you need right at your fingertips, just waiting for you to discover it

Server and Compute Skills

Server and compute skills are one of the core skills of every IT architect. You will be deploying servers in some way shape or form to host everything from application components to hypervisors. It is also important to have a good understanding of how the hardware of a server works, because many of the infrastructure components you will be dealing with build on this concept.

The core components of a server are CPU, RAM, network, and disk (or storage, depending on your use case). Think of some of the other hardware you are going to need to deploy as infrastructure components. For example, a storage array, or a network switch. Each of these infrastructure components share the same underlying server hardware components, even if they are implemented differently underneath the covers.

IT Architect Series: The Journey

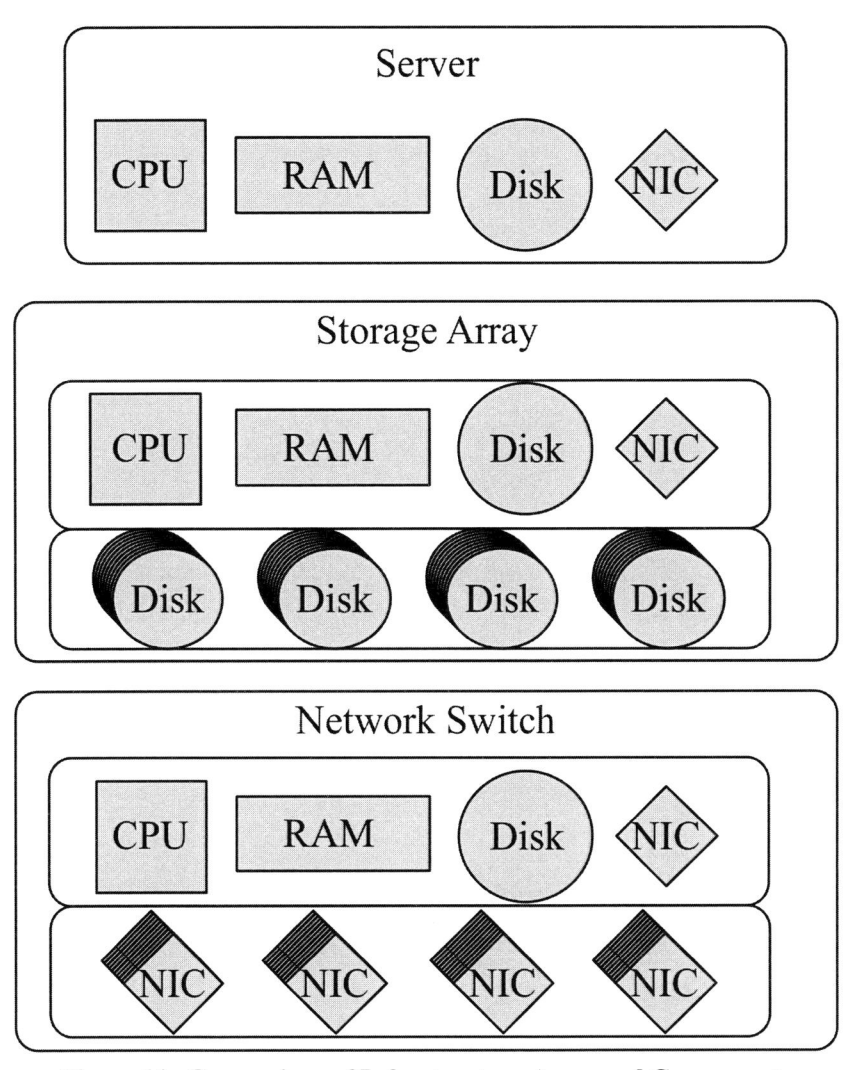

Figure 14 - Comparison of Infrastructure Areas and Components

With the rise of SDE, many are beginning to discount the importance of the hardware underneath. You will hear many software vendors say they **do not care about the hardware it runs on** and **it could be anything**. While this is true to some extent, each vendor will still have CPU, RAM, disk, and network requirements for that hardware no one allegedly cares about. The fact remains, even if you are virtualizing every infrastructure component you can think of, you are still going to need physical hardware at some point.

Gaining Theoretical Knowledge

Pick a server vendor, any server vendor you want. If you go looking around on their website, you will be able to find the technical specifications of the server hardware they make. Pick a model and get acquainted with it. I mean read this thing from cover to cover. You will find out things like what I/O cards are compatible with this hardware, and how the memory is arranged in the banks. Anything you need to know about this piece of hardware is right there. This is still my go-to method for figuring out the specifications (many people refer to specifications as just **specs**) for a server I am working with. I find this much quicker than trying to use any web page to configure what I want, since I am so familiar with these types of documents.

Read about the memory and what speed it operates at. Read about the CPU vendor and family, and what sort of features it has. Read about the storage options you have within the server. Then, when you are comfortable with the model you have picked out, pick another vendor and another model. Once you have done this a few times, you will find these documents much easier to use.

The good news is these documents exist for almost all equipment out there. Also make sure to look at the hardware installation guide, which is another great resource full of useful information.

Gaining Practical Knowledge

The good news is, if you have worked with one server, you have worked with many servers. Servers all consist of the same key components, as we have discussed in detail. The big difference is going to be how you manage the hardware itself, and it becomes even easier to deal with when you have put software on it.

The amount of time you spend with tools the hardware vendor supplies is minimal, in most cases. In the case of rackmount servers, you will be dealing with some sort of baseboard management software. Each vendor has their own software with similar functionality, direct access to the server console for setup, and in case things go horribly, horribly wrong and you cannot access the operating system.

If you have not worked with this, and you cannot manage to get your hands on a server wherever you work for some reason, there is always the eBay special. If you did not already know, eBay is where old hardware goes to die. You can pick up a server for between 100 and 200 US Dollars, more if you want to spend more. One server is enough to run quite a bit on as we further our skills, and if you are willing to purchase a second one you are in very good shape. A word of caution, they generate quite a bit of heat, and use a lot of power, so be prepared for the utility bill which may accompany it.

Once you get your hands on a server, get up close and personal with it. Open it up and take a look. If you are looking at newer servers, you will be surprised at how little is inside of them these days. Over time, servers themselves have become simpler, and the components within them have gotten much smaller.

Virtualization and Virtual Machine Skills

If you know how a server works, you already have a good handle on how a virtual machine works. They share the same components, except a virtual machine's components are well...virtual. Now you are going to have to make sure both your virtual machine and the host is running on both have ample resources.

Gaining Theoretical Knowledge

There is no shortage of ways to get theoretical knowledge out there. There are plenty of books and white papers aimed specifically at virtualization. Reading them is a great place start. VMware, who is one of the premier virtualization software vendors, runs annual conferences called VMworld on their technology which feature conference sessions, labs, and panels. Starting with their latest conferences, VMware has chosen to make these sessions free to view regardless of attending the conference.

Personally, I find conference sessions an excellent way to gain knowledge, especially when they are online and I can access them whenever I want. I cannot even begin to tell you how many hours I have spent watching and listening to material like this. Conference sessions vary in depth from beginner sessions providing high level overviews, to super technical deep-dive sessions for experts. There are sessions that will match your needs on your journey. Many sessions also contain live or recorded demos, which can help to add a little bit of practical knowledge as well. I encourage you to check them out to see what kind of conference resources you can find for your areas of interest.

As for the virtual machines themselves, they are quite like their counterparts, with added flexibility. You can add and remove the virtual hardware components as needed, and some operating systems even let you do this while the virtual machine is running. This is a double-edged sword, since it can be easy to over allocate resources.

One case where this can cause problems is database workloads. Databases can be a critical component to an application, and are being virtualized more and more every single day. They also can have performance issues if their resources are not right sized. This is something someone new to virtualization may not even think about when deploying a database. There are lots of tips and tricks, and yes, best practices around them.

It is important to research the applications and workloads you are virtualizing, to see if there are any special considerations. White papers, books, and blogs are great resources for this. Blogs especially, since many things are learned by trial and error, then documented by bloggers. Blogs are also a great place to go to get an overview of something, without having to sift through a whole book or whitepaper.

Virtual machines are the easy part of virtualization, and the part everyone is most familiar with. The fact is, that virtual machine still runs someplace, and uses all its virtual resources in physical form. There is also the hypervisor software running on the physical server, and its management system. These are key components not to be overlooked in virtualization.

While the hypervisor is what enables the virtual machines to run, the hypervisor management system is what makes the magic happen. Using the example of VMware again, the VMware hypervisor is VMware vSphere ESXi, and the hypervisor management system is VMware vCenter Server. After installing the hypervisor on the physical servers, the hypervisor management system also needs to be installed. A long, long time ago, this also used to be a physical server. Now, it is normal to for it to run on a virtual machine. Why? Simple, the hypervisor management system can protect itself from events like a host hardware failure.

After the management system is built, administrators now can cluster their hypervisor hosts. This is what gives us the ability to protect against things like host hardware failure, and ensure our virtual machines keep running smoothly during periods of resource contention.

To sum it up, you will need to become proficient in the following when learning about virtualization:

- Hypervisor host software (runs on physical server)
- Hypervisor host management system (runs on virtual server)
- Advanced hypervisor host management system features (like those which protect virtual machines)
- Virtual machines

Virtualization is all about protecting the virtual machines and ensuring they are running smoothly. At the end of the day, everything we do as an IT architect is to enable the business needs of our customer.

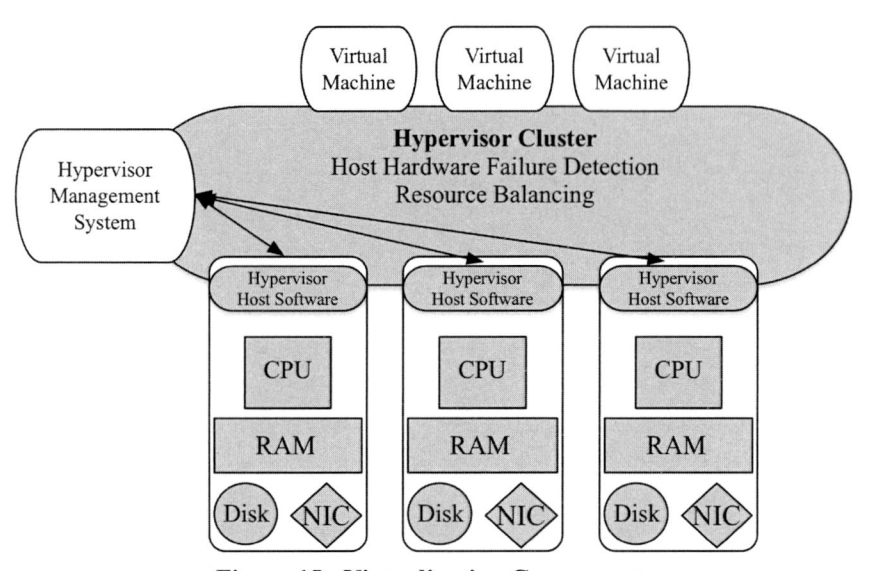

Figure 15 - Virtualization Components

Gaining Practical Knowledge

Remember that computer we talked about earlier? That is more than enough to get you started with some practical hands-on knowledge of virtualization. There are plenty of different ways to get started building your home lab, some automated, and some manual. Before you put in the effort to automate you builds (which can have quite a bit of value!), I encourage you to build the environment manually at least once. Setting up an environment completely is not something we get to do every day. It is good to flex those hands-on muscles, and make sure your skills do not get too rusty. This is another topic that has many of blog articles written about it.

Remember, virtualization is about much more than virtual machines, and it is hard to understand that until you set up a virtualized environment yourself. If you are a virtualization end user, you are missing out on all the fun stuff. By building your own environment, you will get to configure it all, and understand it better than you have before.

Network Skills

The first thing you will realize if you have ever talked to anyone who is involved in networking is that it is always the network. Ok, well it is not always the network, especially if you have a good network team, but the network is usually blamed first for an issue.

The network is often singled out first because it is such a crucial component to today's infrastructure. Without a network, your data center just becomes an expensive heater. Because the network is so critical, the smallest misconfiguration can wreak havoc in any number of places. Remember our example of jumbo frames earlier? There are many more examples of common network issues like this.

Fear not, with a little work, you will be able to ensure you do not encounter these issues, or at least you will know how to recognize them and fix them quickly when they happen.

Gaining Theoretical Knowledge

Network certifications are a big deal. I am not saying you need to run out and get them, but it means there is a great deal of study material already out there. You would be silly not to look at it, even if you do not want to become certified. If you are really lost, pick up a certification guide to one of the Cisco associate level network certifications, such as CCNA. There is a special bonus here, since there are several different flavors of the CCNA. CCNA Routing and Switching is the classic network variation, but there are also CCNA certifications focusing on Security, Data Center, Cloud, and Collaboration. See if you can find a deal where you can pick up a couple of the CCNA guides bundled together for a discount.

Another resource you are probably overlooking is your local community college. Many community colleges have a computer science department, and there are some more bonuses hidden here. The professors there usually teach a class or two because they are passionate about the subject. I have had some fantastic professors at my local community college. There is nothing like being introduced to a subject by someone who is truly passionate about it. Also, taking a course is a good way to make a commitment to your journey. You will have a predictable schedule of when the class meets, and hopefully you can also set a schedule for your course work. Taking a class is a great way to get yourself in the right mindset.

Look at what kind of computer science classes your local community college teaches, you will probably find networking and database classes at a bare minimum. The other great part of this is there will most likely be a lab for you to work in during your class, which brings me to our next topic.

Gaining Practical Knowledge

The best way to figure out how this stuff works is to take a shot at configuring it. For me, things made much more sense once I set up a Layer 2 environment from start to finish. My advice to those looking to get some hands-on time is start with Layer 2, then work your way up the stack to Layer 3.

If you take a community college class, it may help you get some hands-on experience if the course has a lab component. This is a great way to take some baby steps on your journey, if you find the whole process somewhat intimidating.

If your network team has a lab, they may be willing to let you break some things if you ask nicely. If not, you are probably wondering how you are going to afford all this pricy network equipment. You can stop worrying, because there is a whole business built around this. Welcome to the world of rack rentals.

There are multiple providers out there, but they all do pretty much the same thing. They let you schedule blocks of time where you have a nice rack of equipment for your own personal use. If this sounds intimidating to you, do not worry about that either! Many also offer labs and lab guides, so you can work through the process at your own pace.

If you have already started working on your virtualization skills, you can also put them to work by using a network simulator. Network simulators such as GNS3 (open source) or VIRL (Cisco) allow you to build virtual network topologies, and simulate configuration as well as communication between components. These can also be a great resource to work on your practical networking skills, and will also help you work on your virtualization skills during the setup process.

Storage Skills

Storage skills are of course, foundational to any IT infrastructure design. If someone is not busy blaming the network, they are probably going to point at the storage next. Next to the network team, the storage team are the others who are used to having the finger pointed at them, so they may be a little edgy.

Their concerns are founded. So many applications have some sort of storage component to them, whether it be the storage the database is on or the storage the web server is on. Virtualization compounds this, since all those virtual disks need to live on a physical disk someplace.

In the storage world, you are going to be concerned with two things most of the time: performance and capacity. Occasionally, when you are very lucky, your performance and capacity requirements line up and just work. When you are not so lucky, you will find yourself either performance bound or capacity bound. This is why picking the right disks for a storage array is so important.

You may be brushing this off, since SSDs seem to be the answer to everything these days. They can be the answer to many of your problems, but there are other cases when they do not quite fit the bill. This will usually be a large capacity requirement and a low performance requirement. Big, cheap, slow disks still have their place.

There are a couple of big questions when you are learning to architect a solution with storage in mind. How do you know what kind of disks should be in a storage array? Or how do you if you need to make any modifications to an existing storage array to meet requirements? How do you know when to change the configuration of an array to be more cost effective? These are things experience helps teach.

Gaining Theoretical Knowledge

There are quite a few storage companies out there today, and everyone boasts a different set of features and functionality. However, at their core, many storage arrays share the same qualities. It is about reading and writing data from clients to disks, and each vendor puts their special spin on this. These disks are configured logically in various ways so volumes and LUNs can be served to clients from them. A storage array is just a fancy server with many disks (whether they be spinning or solid state) connected to them. Different vendors also use different terms to mean the same thing, so it can get quite confusing when you are learning.

Congratulations, you are now a storage expert. I am kidding…sort of. I am going to bring up another resource here, which may be somewhat controversial to some. It is called the Gartner Magic Quadrant, and you may have just cringed reading that. If so, bear with me. Luckily for you, there's a Gartner Magic Quadrant for just about everything (I am hoping to make it on the Magic Quadrant for books about becoming an IT architect, keep your fingers crossed for me).

Regardless of what the Magic Quadrant says, it is a great place to get an overview of an industry, and who the key players are. For example, if you do not know anything about storage and are not sure where to start learning, look at a Magic Quadrant, and pick something. You can't go wrong if you are trying to get an understanding of the industry and technologies and you pick from the Magic Quadrant. I am not saying you should design an infrastructure from a random pick off the Magic Quadrant, which would be a horrible idea since the Magic Quadrant does not know anything about your customer's requirements.

When you pick a storage vendor to study, I encourage you to look at the disk types in the array, and then what the vendor suggests the storage array should be used for. I briefly mentioned the three main disk types you will encounter today earlier. They are SATA, SAS, and SSD. While the storage world is rapidly evolving, understanding the characteristics of these drive types will get you started.

SSDs are the fastest out of the drive types, since they do not have any moving parts. When we talk about SATA and SAS drives, SATA drives spin slower and have a higher capacity, and SAS drives spin faster and have a lower capacity. The faster the disks spin, the more input/output operations per second (IOPS), the storage array can push. In the case of SSDs, not spinning at all is even better than the fastest spinning disks available. You will need to weigh these options as an IT architect. In addition, the cost and latency of the disk you will encounter is inversely proportional.

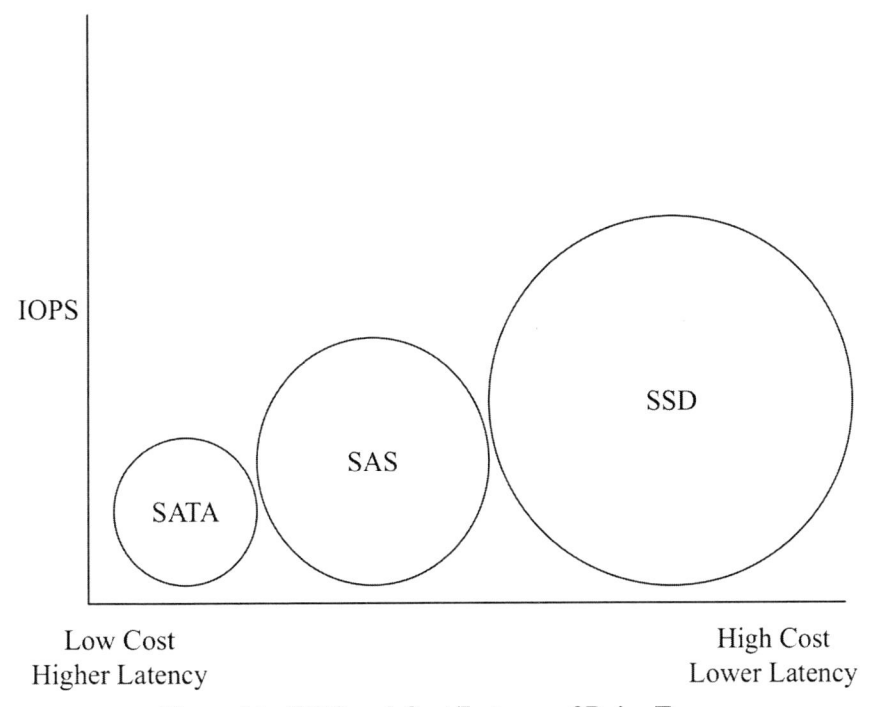

Figure 16 - IOPS and Cost/Latency of Drive Types

In simple terms, think of latency as waiting. You do not like waiting in line, do you? Well neither does anything in the IT infrastructure you are designing. Latency is applicable just about through every component of your infrastructure in different forms. Different applications will have different tolerance levels for latency. In this case, some may be okay waiting for their storage, just a tiny bit, while others are not okay waiting very much at all.

Back to reading about what storage arrays are used for. If you look at enough case studies, which all vendors have in abundance, you will be able to get a feel for when what type of disk is required.

Gaining Practical Knowledge

Practical storage skills can be challenging. After all, you can't really walk into the local electronics store and buy an enterprise storage array. The good news is vendors know this, and they want to get their technology into prospective customer's hands easily. Many vendors have simulators of their storage arrays that will run just fine in your lab.

You cannot expect much in the way of performance, but you can get some good hands on understanding of what it takes to configure and manage a storage array. Pick your favorite storage vendor (or the one they use where you work) and seek out their simulator.

Your storage team is also an invaluable resource. Remember I mentioned my trick about volunteering for storage maintenance? You should try it. You can learn a lot by simply sitting with the storage team as they do their normal thing. This is the tactic I used when I first started learning about storage.

Application Skills

These skills can be difficult to get a handle on, because you never know what sort of application you may be architecting an IT infrastructure for. Application skills also tie back to virtual machine skills, since different applications may have different virtualization requirements.

You can learn as many applications as you want right now, but I guarantee you will encounter something you have never heard of at some point. Let's talk about gaining application skills in general terms, since it is something you will be dealing with repeatedly.

Gaining Theoretical Knowledge

The first step of learning an application is to put it in terms which make sense for you. This is one thing I have found very helpful to me during my journey, not just for applications, but for anything I am trying to make sense of. If you can come at the skill you are trying to obtain from a direction you are already familiar with, this will make it much easier to pick up.

For a long time, I tied everything back to virtualization, and I mean everything. Let's take the example of an Apache web server. While it is not an overly complex system, it is widely used. There is not much to do if I need a new web server. First, I create a new virtual machine and install an operating system. Then, I install the apache package followed by configuration of the folder location and default web page. Sure, it is a rudimentary web server, but it is a web server. I need to ensure it is created with the appropriate virtual hardware, and virtual network components. If I had to deal with creating a physical web server, this same process would hold true, except I would have much less flexibility with my hardware components. This process also got me some practical knowledge if configured myself a web server in a virtual environment.

The biggest skill I learned in this method was storage. There was a point where I did not know much about storage. I only knew I never wanted anything that was on a SATA array for my VMware ESXi hosts. I could also add storage to my VMware vSphere cluster, but that was about it. When I found myself needing to learn storage quickly, I dove in and learned everything I could about storage for VMware ESXi. By the time I was ready to start addressing the physical aspects of the storage array, I was much more comfortable with these aspects since I understood how they related to VMware ESXi. This method works for anything you want to learn, especially if you are willing to be a little creative.

It is also worth noting that most application vendors also have best practices and white papers describing how to configure their application for specific use cases. These will be a great first step when you are tasked with learning a new application.

Gaining Practical Knowledge

Sometimes, applications can be a little tricky to get hands on experience with, depending on where you are in your organization at work. Often, application and infrastructure teams are under separate business units, with a liaison in between. You may not be able to get the all clear to go spend time digging in with an application team. If you can, great, if not, don't sweat it.

Remember, we just talked about relating things to what you are comfortable with. If you are a network person, get a handle on the network profile of the application. Find out things about when the servers are transmitting the most data, and when they are not transmitting very much at all. Learning an application's network performance protocol can help you learn how it behaves, and what it does. Let's pretend the following is a graph of network performance.

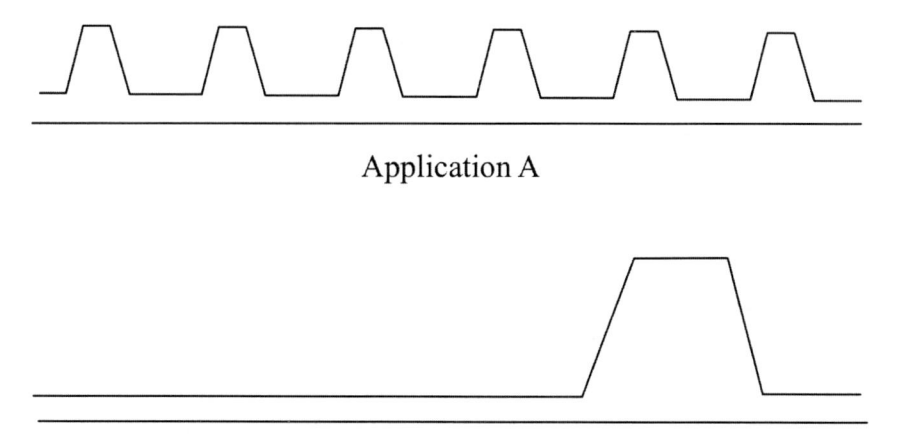

Application A

Application B

Figure 17 - Network Throughput Diagram

This graph was created on the last day of the month. As you can see, Application A seems to be transmitting a lot of data on a regular time interval, say 30 minutes. Application B transmitted a lot of data once on the last day of the month, and when we checked the graphs for the rest of the month we did not see a lot of traffic. This means Application A is quite busy. We should dive into what this traffic really is. It may be some sort of replication mechanism, meaning Application A could be important, or, it could just be chatty because of the way it was written.

Application B on the other hand does not seem to do that much, except for the last day of the month. This does not mean we should discount the criticality of Application B, it may perform some sort of month end financial analysis. It could also replicate something once a month. There are many functions these applications may perform. If you are a network person, this can be your starting point for learning more about either of these applications. By using their network profile, you can begin to determine what the applications do, and what other infrastructure components they impact.

Backup and Recovery Skills

When we talk about backup and recovery skills, the backup tool you are using is not nearly as important as the policies around the backups. It would be nice if you could get your hands on one or two popular tools and take them for a drive around the block.

Gaining Theoretical Knowledge

The best place to start gaining theoretical knowledge is your own organization. Find out some of the backup policies in use today, and start from there.

Remember, backups must live someplace at the end of the day, and the space backups consume is not free. Because of this, you will often see different backup policies for different types of data. Most organizations will categorize the servers and data in a variety of ways, and often will use different terms for how they achieve this. Some popular ones are **class** or **tier**. For this example, let's think of a customer who has three tiers in their environment.

Table 7 - Thirty M Three, Inc. Tiers of Service

Thirty M Three, Inc. Tiers of Service	
Tier	**Purpose**
1	Production
2	Development
3	Test

If Tier 1 is Production, chances are the policies it uses for backup and recovery will be different than the Development and Test tiers. Unless of course, Thirty M Three, Inc. does a huge amount of development work. Then, their development environment may become much more critical. This also may tie in very closely with Thirty M Three's Business Continuity and Disaster Recovery planning. As you can see, it is very important for an IT architect to understand the applications and the workloads in the environment they are creating.

There are a thousand people out there who all have different ideas of what an organization's backup policy should be. It is up to you, as an IT architect, to work with your customers to decide which suits their business needs.

Gaining Practical Knowledge

If we are talking about the backup and recovery tools themselves, there are a few vendors who offer free trials or NFR licenses. One which comes to mind quickly is Veeam Backup & Replication. Veeam's documentation is also top notch, and will get you up and running quickly. This of course does not mean you will be using their software for every environment you design. It is also important to look at the other vendors in the marketplace.

Another good place to get started is your own environment. Do some research and see if you can find out how your organization backs up their data, and how they classify this. With any luck, you will be able to do this as part of a project you are working on. Make a note of the different types of data, and how they are backed up in the environment. Also, do not forget to find out how long the recovery of the data will take. This will tie in to the next thing we are going to discuss.

Business Continuity and Disaster Recovery Skills

Business Continuity and Disaster Recovery are often overlooked in many environments, simply because a company has never faced a disaster and had to recover from it. Many have learned the hard way this is a critical piece of their infrastructure planning, and have never recovered. It is important to remember downtime costs customers money, how much depends on what type of business they are in, as well as the length and the time of the outage. This is why a good IT architect always includes Business Continuity and Disaster Recovery in an IT infrastructure design.

Gaining Theoretical Knowledge

There is a very big line between theoretical and practical knowledge for this skill set. Just because we have a business continuity and disaster recovery plan in place, it does not mean we know it will work until we test it, which is a very practical application.

Depending on the criticality of the data, you may be using the backups we just talked about to recover in the case of a disaster. The tools you use to protect and restore your data will depend on the SLA the environment needs to provide, as well as the RTO and RPO for the environment, among other things.

Now what if you walk into a customer, and they do not have any idea of what these things mean? In this case, you are going to have to walk your customer through a BIA to determine how much downtime is acceptable to the business, and what the cost is.

Remember the conversation we had about academics before? This is one of those areas which you can also benefit from some academic training if these concepts are completely foreign to you. Business Continuity and Disaster Recovery are hot topics in the world of IT infrastructure. Your local community college most likely has a course covering these topics, and there are numerous text books out there covering it. These topics is they may be covered as part of a business or a technology academic program. In many cases, courses like this are cross-listed between both areas.

Gaining Practical Knowledge

The best thing you can possibly do is take part in a disaster recovery test. If this is not already part of your job, make sure you volunteer for this one, you will not want to miss this learning opportunity. I am not going to lie, disaster recovery tests are not a favorite of most people, especially when they are multiday affairs.

Beyond being involved in a test itself, the team responsible for business continuity and disaster recovery is a great resource. When you explain to them you want to make sure your piece of the environment adheres to the company standards, they will most likely be more than willing to explain how the plans were created, and the business reasons behind them.

Even if Business Continuity and Disaster Recovery is not in the scope of your job today, you can keep it in your mind. To further work on these skills, you can come up with your own Business Continuity and Disaster Recovery plans for whatever projects you are working on. For example, if you are a storage administrator today, I am sure you are used to getting many, many requests attached to projects. If you cannot get more information about a project and its specific business requirements and criticality, invent it on your own for practice. There is nothing stopping you from doing your own BIA, and assigning your own SLA, then protecting the application accordingly. Remember, a notebook is a great place to keep these imaginary projects as you progress on your journey. This way you can look back on it later, and see how far you have really come.

Security Skills

Security is one of the hottest topics around in this day and age. You hear about data breech after data breach, and you never want your customers to be one of the victims. It is up to you, as the IT architect, to keep in mind security as you architect your design. Depending on the industry of your customer, they may already have very stringent security requirements you must adhere to. In other environments, it may be up to you to work with the customer to determine what their security requirements really are.

Gaining Theoretical Knowledge

Once again, certifications are a big deal in security, and there are quite a few them. One of the most popular certifications is the Certified Information Systems Security Professional or CISSP. This certificate is no joke, and has several requirements you must meet before you can even take the exam. The good news is there are many resources out there to study for this exam, which will help you get an understanding of the security arena.

Remember, when it comes to certification exams, there is always a map to help get you started. Different vendors call it different things. In the case of the CISSP exam, it is called the Exam Outline, but many other vendors refer to it as an exam blueprint. These documents are a great resource for topics to study as part of your journey.

A security class at your local community college is also a great starting point for this part of the journey. Have I mentioned many community colleges also have online classes? This can be a more flexible option if you are not sold on going to campus. Make sure to read the fine print, since many professors run their online courses a different way. Some will have a required weekly class meeting, or some will follow a self-paced model with assignments due on a consistent basis. It may take a couple of shots for you to find out what type of online class works for you, or if online classes work for you at all.

Gaining Practical Knowledge

You probably already know I am going to suggest you speak to your security team at work to find out what kind of security measures your company already takes, and you may not be thrilled. Many security teams have a sort of hard exterior, mainly because they are used to people coming to them and asking for exceptions from policies. When you show them you want to work with them, not against them, you will see a world of difference. Your security team can become one of your greatest learning resources.

Strengthening Your Foundation

It is important to keep these technologies in mind, and how they impact each other during the journey. It is also important to keep in mind is how the technologies you are using in your design relate to the existing infrastructure, and the complete solution. Take a step back and think about common factors for all the technologies you will be touching as an IT architect. First and foremost, we need to make sure we meet our customer's requirements, and mitigate any risks we discover in the process.

After we have taken care meeting our customer's business requirements, we need to be concerned about things across the various infrastructure areas. For example, we should be concerned with how a component will react in the event of the failure of a different component. Will the environment remain operational? At what point will we need to invoke Disaster Recovery plans? We will also need to be concerned with how easy things will be for our customer after we hand over their brand-new environment for them. Are we using technologies they have no experience with? If so, how are we ensuring their success? What about their applications? Are they meeting their end user's requirements? How do we measure the load on the environment, and when do we expected performance degradation to begin? In this day and age of constant security breaches, how have we protected our customer across their infrastructure components?

If we sit down and think about most of these questions, we can answer them with these little things called the design qualities.

Table 8 - Infrastructure Design Quality Ranking

	Rank	Design Quality
Most Important	1	Availability
	2	Manageability
	3	Security
	4	Performance
Least Important	5	Recoverability

IT Architect Series: The Journey

In the table above, I have ranked the design qualities in no particular order. As an IT architect, you are going to work with your customer to determine which design qualities are the most and least important to them, and rank them accordingly. You can then apply these qualities appropriately when you make design choices. In the example above, Manageability is more important to the customer than Security. In this case, you may choose not to implement security features which would cause management overhead, but you would certainly document the risk of not applying them.

Introduction to Design Choices

We are going to talk much more about design choices a little later, but I want to introduce them to you now so you can begin to frame your thinking in these terms. You may also hear IT architects talk about something called design decisions. Personally, I prefer to call them design choices, because as IT architects, everything we do is a choice for one reason or another to meet our customer's business needs.

When we make a design choice, there are many things we must consider as an IT architect. Beyond considering business requirements, a design choice may also be the result of a constraint the project has upon it. These choices we make as IT architects also will have an impact on one or more of these design qualities.

For example, when we make the physical design choice of choosing a storage array model, we are usually basing our choice on more than what is on sale from a vendor that week. Our storage array choice will impact other areas of our infrastructure, so we want to make sure it is resilient in the case of some sort of component failure. A component failure could impact the **availability** of our environment. We also want to make sure the data on our storage array is backed up or replicated in accordance to its criticality. Any number of component failures, including our storage array being eaten by zombies could impact the **recoverability** of our environment. The choice of this storage array has cascading implications throughout the design of our infrastructure.

Melissa Palmer

On Our Way

These technology skills are not going to be learned overnight. Like anything else, they will take time and practice. When you create your learning plan for each skill, do not be afraid to change the order as needed. Sometimes we just get stuck in a certain area. Instead of burning time on something that just is not making sense to you right now, or you are not excited about, move on to something else for the meantime. I have often found that if I put something down for a while, and come back to it later, it makes much more sense the second time when I look at it with a fresh perspective.

Another strategy for ensuring you put the needed time into the areas you are not as fond of is bribery. Bribe yourself to do it. Create a time exchange for yourself. For example, for every two hours of working with the topics you dread, reward yourself with 30 minutes of something fun. Reading a magazine, playing a game, or just surfing the Internet. This strategy helps to make the unbearable a bit more palatable.

This does not, however, mean you should wait until near the end of your journey to address these infrastructure areas. For a very long time, I dreaded dealing with Backup and Recovery. I mean, absolutely dreaded it. It had brought me nothing but headaches for as long as I could remember, so it was not anything I was very excited about.

At heart, many of us are technologists. That is why we are embarking on this journey in the first place. If a technologist does not like a technology, there is usually a reason. One reason is the specific products you have been exposed to. I do not want to name names, but let me just say the backup products I had been working with for a very long time were not designed with virtualization in mind, which is why, of course, they made my life miserable. Once I found the right products out there, and spent time with them, it changed my perspective on this technology. Now, I have completely changed my mindset and love working with Backup and Recovery products after I have been introduced to the right ones.

Another reason we do not like technologies is sometimes the people we associate with them. Lucky for me, even when backups were driving me nuts, the people I worked with to fix them were very, very nice. If this was not the case I would probably have hated it even more. This is why it is important for us to step back as IT architects, and figure out what really is fueling our dislike of something. Especially when it is something we know will be important as we continue the IT architecture journey.

The Lesson May Be Hidden

As with the rest of our journey, there is always something to learn from the adventures we have. In these cases, when we have an aversion to something, the lesson may be hidden. If we find a situation incredibly different to learn from, the lesson may simply be not to do it the way we have been doing it.

If we have struggled with a piece of technology by ourselves, the lesson may be to ask a friend or mentor for experience. If we have struggled on the outside of a situation looking in, the lesson may be to stand up and say something. Sometimes the most powerful lesson you can learn from another person is what not to do.

CHAPTER 9

PUTTING TOGETHER THE ARCHITECTURAL BUILDING BLOCKS

"It is difficult to say what is impossible, for the dream of yesterday is the hope of today and the reality of tomorrow."
— *Robert H. Goddard*

If we thought of creating an IT architecture in the way we did constructing a building, the architectural building blocks would be the things you need to make the building functional. Sure, you could open a building without thing like window coverings, lights, flooring or interior walls, but you would not be able to do much with it. Your client has a very specific use case in mind for their new space. If you do not provide what they are looking for, they are left with a massive investment they cannot even use. This could spell disaster for any business, no matter how big or small it is. Would you have office cubicles in a restaurant space? Would you have an office without restrooms? Of course not. One could argue you could create an IT infrastructure without taking any of these building blocks into account, but you would not necessarily have an IT infrastructure which was functional for your customer at the end of the day.

Continue Building

Since we have now connected the infrastructure areas of expertise, it is time to put together the architectural building blocks. I hope your walking shoes are comfortable, because we still have many steps to go together on our journey.

Can you design an IT architecture purely based on the technologies you prefer? Of course you can. Can you design an IT architecture based on some random technologies you have picked out of a box, or which were on sale this week? Of course you can. Can you build an IT architecture with a bunch of old equipment which no longer has an active service contract? Of course you can. However, just because you can, does not mean you should.

Being an IT architect is so much more than sticking a bunch of technology together and having it work. Is that a big part of the job? Absolutely. Is it difficult? Of course. It will not be difficult due to your technical abilities, or your understanding of technology. It will be difficult because your job as an IT architect is to design a solution which meets your customer's requirements and needs.

The Architectural Building Blocks

We have talked a little about the building blocks you will need to put together to become an IT architect, beyond your technology skillset:

- Gathering Requirements
- Determining Constraints
- You Know What They Say About Assumptions
- Identifying and Managing Risks
- Project Planning
- Procurement and Vendor Management
- Public Presenting and Speaking
- Written Communication

I hope these skills will become second nature to you, and you are beginning to understand how important they are to your role as an IT architect.

When we want to build these skills, we can begin by leveraging the learning tools we have now discovered. As I have mentioned before, getting experience in these areas sometimes is not as cut and dry as it is with a technical skill. Sometimes it is harder to measure our progress with these softer skills due their nature. It is not as easy as configuring a piece of software, or connecting two different pieces of hardware.

The Conceptual Model Revisited

We touched a bit on the conceptual model earlier, and we are now getting ready to visit it again. The good news is some of the skills we are working on here will help you to develop a conceptual design for an IT architecture. For many (myself included) this is one of the harder concepts to grasp on the journey. It is also the most important first step to architect any IT environment you step into.

Working on the skills related to developing a conceptual design is a great opportunity to work with others, whether it be a mentor, or other aspiring IT architects. The more you talk through these concepts with others, the more they will start to make sense. The experience of others can also help you develop your personal methods for creating the conceptual model for your IT infrastructure designs.

We are going to talk about our first four architectural building blocks, then continue with our discussion of the conceptual model, and how these building blocks come together to create the walls of the building we are creating. When you understand the infrastructure areas of expertise and the architectural building blocks, it becomes easier to put together a complete structure. In this case, the structure is the IT architecture design for our customer.

Gathering Requirements

Business driven requirements are key to any IT architect's success. These requirements are why we exist in the first place. You would think this would be easy, because the customer is always right, right? Wrong. A big part of your job as an IT architect is to ensure your customers are doing things for the right reason. For example, let's say your customer requires a SLA of 99.999%. By the way, that translates to five minutes of unplanned downtime per year. It is up to you to find out why, exactly, the customer thinks they need this kind of availability. There could of course, be a legitimate business reason, such as they will lose $10 Million dollars' worth of manufacturing capacity for five minutes of downtime. On the other hand, they may just have asked for five nines of availability since they read something on the Internet which said they needed it.

When a customer tells you what their requirement is, as an IT architect, it is your job to determine what is driving that requirement from a business perspective. After you understand the requirement, it is your job to meet the requirement with the sole purpose of enabling that business function.

For those of us who are true lovers of technology, this can be hard at first. Let's go back to our example of the SuperUltraExa hypervisor. Perhaps you have been working with the SuperUltraExa hypervisor in your lab for some time, or even at a previous position. Currently, the company you work at now uses the DonkeyExpress hypervisor. They have been using DonkeyExpress for some time. Their business processes are aligned with it, their staff is trained in it, but you feel SuperUltraExa would be a better solution for the organization.

Get ready for an uphill battle. I am not saying you will not be able to pull off convincing the company to switch hypervisors, but you will need the business data to back it up. Here are some things you should be thinking of:

- What business advantage does SuperUltraExa have over DonkeyExpress? What features does SuperUltraExa have that DonkeyExpress does not, and how can the organization use them to its advantage?
- Is there any cost savings to adopting SuperUltraExa over DonkeyExpress?
- What would be the cost of switching to SuperUltraExa? Even if licensing is cheaper, do not forget about the human cost of re-training staff and changing Standard Operating Procedures (SOPs) and processes.

These are the types of things you should begin to think about. Simply saying SuperUltraExa is better is not going to get you anywhere. You always need the business case to back up your technology choices.

Gaining Theoretical Knowledge

It would be great if we received a magical list of requirements from our customers, and got right to designing, right? The good news is sometimes this happens, such as in an RFP situation. The bad news is the solution you design for RFP requirements probably will not match what you ultimately deploy. Customers like to do something called an **apples to apples** comparison where they make everyone design for the same set of sometimes off the wall requirements.

There are a couple of places you can encounter this and benefit from it. If you know your company will be issuing an IT infrastructure RFP sometime soon, ask for a copy of it. Better yet, ask if you can sit in on some of the meetings developing it. The learning opportunity here is both theoretical and practical, which we will expand on shortly.

When I was a Systems Engineer, I was the RFP queen. I really, really enjoyed responding to them. As a customer, I liked seeing all the different responses from the vendors. RFPs are a great opportunity to flex those design muscles, whatever side of the fence you are on.

Gaining Practical Knowledge

I want to start by reminding you of one of the learning methods I mentioned earlier, the Socratic Method. When you find yourself with a customer who has not yet determined their concrete requirements (perhaps they do not even understand what their requirements are), the Socratic Method can help you lead a discussion with them to refine those requirements. Getting everyone in a room talking is often the first step in determining the requirements and creating a conceptual design. This is also something the customer may not have done before you were brought in. Sometimes customers need an external authoritative force to bring them together, and this force is you, the IT architect.

If there is an RFP going out where you work, and you have been involved in the meetings for it, or have a copy of it, answer it. You probably think I am crazy if you have ever read a hundred page RFP response. You do not need to go into that level of detail, but as an aspiring IT architect you should be looking for every opportunity you can get your hands on to build those IT architecture muscles for the journey forward.

Another simple thing to do is break every task you do at work into requirements. Think of every single project you touch in the manner of what business problem you are trying to solve. This may take some research on your part, but it will be worth your time and effort.

Finally, start to pay close attention on what happens during a project kickoff meeting. Chances are they will be talking about requirements, even if they are not specifically calling them by name. Everything is done for a reason, it is up to you as an IT architect to determine those reasons, as well as what needs to be done to ensure those reasons become a reality.

Determining Constraints

Constraints can look quite a bit like requirements when you are first beginning your IT architecture journey. After you have several requirements discovered, you should then ensure they are, in fact, really requirements instead of constraints. Remember, constraints will impact your ability to design the infrastructure, and cannot be easily changed. For example, a customer may tell you specifically not to use a certain vendor, because they have had a bad experience with them in the past, and refuse to do further business with them. While this reason is not technical, it is still very valid to your customer.

Constraints must also be evaluated, as they can also lead to risks. When a risk is identified, it must also be mitigated. We will talk about risks shortly.

Gaining Theoretical Knowledge

There are several definitions for the word **constrain** according to our friends at Merriam-Webster. For our purposes, the definition "to force by imposed structure, restriction, or limitation" is the most applicable. A big part of understanding what constraints are is understanding why they are constraints in the environment you are working with.

For example, a customer may tell you an existing storage array must be used. This may seem frustrating to you, since you want to pick the storage array which will fit the customer's requirements in the best possible way.

The customer could be using an existing array for any number of reasons, which can be technical or business related. Cost may be a factor. If the array is already deployed on the floor, they will not need to purchase it. There may also be operational constraints, since your customer's staff may already be proficient in the management tools for the specific array. Although you already know must use this array, you still must perform an evaluation on it. The array could be brand new and recently purchased, or it could be aging with an expired support contract.

Gaining Practical Knowledge

It can take some time to become comfortable with the idea of constraints. The best way to start getting comfortable is to start working with them. What are the constraints the current projects you are working on? What are some of your constraints on a Friday night? The more you start to use the concepts that make up the conceptual model, the easier it will become to do it.

If we go back to our storage array example, we really need to take things a step further than we did when we were talking about the theoretical knowledge of constraints. Knowing you need to use an array and what it looks like on paper is one thing. Beyond simply ensuring the array is under a valid support contract, you must take things a step further. Will this storage array have enough capacity, in both space and performance for your environment? Does the storage array currently have any periods when it runs at high utilization? Can your storage array meet the latency requirements of your application? These are all things which become very practical when dealing with constraints.

You Know What They Say About Assumptions

We all know what they say about assumptions, especially after our discussion on assumptions earlier. Not only is documenting assumptions important as an IT architect, but it is important in many other areas of life. Do you assume you are having chicken for dinner tonight, or do you know you are having chicken for dinner tonight? If you want chicken, but you are not the one cooking dinner, there is a chance chicken may not be on your plate that evening. If you assume you are having chicken for dinner tonight, you had better check with whoever is in charge of preparing the meal if you really want chicken. You risk not having chicken on your plate if you do not validate that assumption. Assumptions also can lead to traps. If we are used to something happening on a regular basis, we may assume it. If you have had chicken for dinner every Monday for the last three months, you may assume you are having it every Monday night. This may lead to disappointment when there is something other than chicken your plate next Monday.

Sure, this chicken analogy is silly, especially if you are reading this and do not eat chicken. It is, however, a good illustration of how assumptions can lead to problems, in everyday life and in your life as an IT architect.

Gaining Theoretical Knowledge

First, I want you to think about a time an assumption caused trouble for you. We can all think of at least one time it did. For example, I know it used to take me 35 minutes to get to my office if I left my house at a certain time. On most days, I would simply assume this, and carry on as normal. However, the highway I travelled on was notorious for accidents, and since I assumed it would take me 35 minutes to get to work, I never checked the traffic unless I knew I had to be there early for a specific reason. This of course, lead to conference calls in the car several times when something went wrong during my commute. Most days, this was a risk I was willing to take. On days where I knew I had to be there at a certain time, I would not assume my normal travel time, I would keep an eye on the traffic.

I want you to make a list of times you assumed things, like how I used to assume my commute. Then, I want you to list any risks you incurred with these assumptions. You already know them, since you have already encountered them.

Then, I want you to think about things you are assuming currently which are not as obvious. This could be things which are part of your journey to becoming an IT architect, or things in everyday life. Then, document the risks associated with them, and how you can mitigate those risks.

Exercises like this will help you in your IT architecture journey. The biggest mental jump on the journey after you have gotten experience in the infrastructure areas of expertise and the architecture building blocks is thinking like an IT architect. Incorporating practice into your daily routine makes the jump a lot easier.

Gaining Practical Knowledge

Now that you have practiced identifying assumptions, it is time to put this skill into use. I want you to make a list of current projects you are involved in at work, and the assumptions you are working under for each project. Hopefully these assumptions already been documented as part of the project, but if not, this is excellent opportunity to make sure they are. Talk them over with your team members to get more input on them, and how others see these assumptions. If you do discover anything earthshattering, it may be a good idea to bring them to the attention of your manager or friendly neighborhood project manager, who we will talk about in a little while.

Now, there is also an opportunity for some fun here. When someone is talking about an assumption on a project you are working on in a meeting, there is nothing wrong with bringing it up. You can always nicely ask what they are basing their assumption on, and if there is any risk involved. Doing this has the potential to make a boring meeting much more interesting, and make sure assumptions do not negatively impact a project.

Identifying and Managing Risks

I hate to be the bringer of the dark cloud over your head, but risks are everywhere we look, especially when designing an IT infrastructure. We just talked about assumptions, and the risks they can add to a project, but this is not the only place you will encounter risk in a project. You think you are solving a problem by replacing your customer's out of support hardware with nice, new shiny hardware by a different vendor, right? Of course you are, but you are also introducing a risk, by bringing an unknown element into the infrastructure. It is up to you, as an IT architect, to mitigate these risks as you introduce them into your customer's environment.

Gaining Theoretical Knowledge

I have always found the mitigation of the risks introduced as the result of a design choice the easiest ones to identify and fix. It is also easy to go overboard and find a risk in every single design choice you make, even when you have already mitigated it someplace else. Risk management is a certainly a balance between being over cautious, and not cautious enough.

The harder risks to determine and mitigate are those inherent to your project. For example, let's say you are tasked with putting a new virtualization environment in one of your customer's data centers. This seems innocuous enough, after all, who does not want a brand-new virtualization environment? As an IT architect, it us up to you to dig a little deeper beneath the surface of this seemingly harmless request. Later, you find out your customer is currently running production in not one, but two of their data centers, with each data center serving as its partner's disaster recovery site.

Your customer's requirement of a new virtualization environment in only one of the two sites introduces a risk, as you won't have a new environment in the partner site to recover to. In the event of a disaster, your customer's new workloads could be in big trouble. It is up to you, as the IT architect, to come up with a solution to mitigate this risk, which may take some creativity in this case. Even if your customer accepts the risk, which may be the case, it is up to you as the IT architect to provide them with a mitigation, even if they choose not to implement it right now.

There is a wealth of knowledge available out there about IT risk management. Risk management is a big part of process management and improvement frameworks such as ITIL or Six Sigma. If you are not used to working with risks, this is a good place to start getting some more exposure. Your local community college also more than likely has a course on business risk management just waiting for you to enroll in, you may even be able to find an IT centric risk management course.

Gaining Practical Knowledge

The example I gave above is a more business-related risk. When you are working with technology, start thinking of some of the technology issues you deal with on a day to day basis as risks. For example, if your network switch has two redundant power supplies, and one fails, what risk has been introduced into your environment, and how can it be mitigated? After you have done a little bit more research on risks, pick a project you are working on and make two lists: one of the business-related risks, and one of the technology-related risks. Start doing this for every project you work on, and compare the lists periodically. You will see your understanding of infrastructure design risks evolving as you compare notes.

The best thing you can do for something like understanding risk management to work with someone who already understands it, whether it be a mentor, or a co-worker. We are about to introduce your friendly neighborhood project manager, who would be an excellent resource to work with. If you want to make sure you have a clear understanding of what the risks are on your current and future projects, this person is a good place to start.

Conceptual to Logical to Physical

The first four architectural building blocks we talked about are combined create the conceptual design of an IT infrastructure project. After an IT architect has created the conceptual design for a project, they can then proceed to creating the logical design and physical design for the project. The conceptual design is one of the most important parts of an IT infrastructure project, since the logical and physical designs are built on top of it. A change to the conceptual design will certainly have a chain reaction effect, changing the logical and physical designs for the IT infrastructure.

After the creation of the conceptual design, many IT architects will hold meetings with their customer to go through the design line by line. This is to ensure everyone is on the same page, and to make sure the IT architect has a solid foundation to continue to build their logical design and physical design on top of. No matter how diligent the IT architect, the fact remains sometimes the conceptual design will change later in a project. As we all know, the customer is always right, even when they are not. As such, it is important to remember to document risks as they arise in a project, no matter what phase a project is in. Changing the conceptual design midway through a project certainly has the potential to introduce additional risk.

Logical Then Physical

Since many IT architects are also technologists, many of us want to jump straight to the technology after finishing the conceptual model. Remember, the logical design does not contain specific vendors or specific technologies, it is the definition of the technical and operational capabilities we need to meet our customer's requirements. After the conceptual design has been created, your next big task as an IT architect is to create the logical model. If you read only the logical design of an IT infrastructure, you would have a good understanding of how it worked. You would understand

After the creation of the logical design, it is time to create the physical design. At this point, you will begin choosing the vendors and technologies which are going to be used to solve your customer's business problems. The physical design will tell you the very specific detail of how those technical and operational capabilities are being implemented in this IT infrastructure environment.

The logical and physical designs are very distinct, but still related to each other. Your logical design will drive your physical design. If you have determined you are segregating network traffic by VLANs in your logical design, the physical design will be how those VLANs are implemented. While many technology products do have specific features and functionality, the fact is multiple products should be able to be used to implement the logical design.

Let's say you have implemented an IT infrastructure for your customer, and they want to deploy the same infrastructure in a different site, with one small change. Unfortunately, your customer has had a terrible experience with their BackFlip Sideways (which is not a real vendor) network switches over the last year, and they want to us a different vendor for this new site. This will change your physical network design. Your logical network design will remain the same, as you will be providing the same technical and operational capabilities with the new switch vendor you choose. What will change is the implementation of these capabilities, or your physical design.

Now, let's return to our regularly scheduled discussion on the architectural building blocks.

Project Planning

Before we even get started, I must admit this is one of my least favorite architectural building blocks. I do not have an explanation why other than it just is not my thing. That does not mean I did not have to go ahead and learn it anyway, because I did. We all have areas on our journey that we do not particularly like, but that does not mean we can avoid walking with them along the journey.

I think the problem I had with project planning and project management was, well, interaction with bad project managers. Luckily, later in my career I encountered some good ones. Unfortunately, the damage was already done. This is probably one of the reasons I am leading with calling it project planning instead of project management. While the ideas are of course very similar, to me project planning means understanding all phases of the project completely, something you will have to do as an IT architect. From gathering requirements, to turning over the environment post production, a good IT architect needs to understand how all the phases of the project are planned, and of course managed.

Gaining Theoretical Knowledge

There is no shortage of information on project management theory out there, so the good news is this is one of the easier topics to gain theoretical knowledge on. Start out by doing some reading on project management methodologies, and try to think which ones would be work best in your organization right now. Make a list, and then do further research on each of them.

I hope you have a favorite project manager, because I know I usually do. At this point, seek them out and ask about their experience with these methodologies. Also ask them what they prefer to subscribe to, and why.

Remember how we talked about certifications being a good study tool for technical resources? There is also a popular project management certification called Project Management Professional (PMP) by the Project Management Institute. Studying for this certification provides a good overview of project management processes, even if you have no intention of taking the exam. I have looked at study material for the PMP, and found it helpful, but I never have been interested in going further than that, and obtaining the certification.

Gaining Practical Knowledge

The best way to get practical knowledge in project planning is, well, to plan a project of course. The next time you start a project, think of the different project management methodologies you have studied. Pick one, and try to implement it. You may not pick the correct one at first, and that is quite alright. Pick another, and try again.

The various project management methodologies encompass many of the same principles, which you can begin to apply in your project work. As you get started, make sure you pay attention to things like dependencies, timelines, and resource constraints. These are usually the things that can bring a project to a screeching halt. I encourage you to document these things on your next project to begin flexing those project management muscles.

Procurement and Vendor Management

Though you may have vendors you like the most, the vendors you pick as you create the physical design for your customer will depend on their requirements, or even their constraints. Even if DonkeyExpress is your favorite hypervisor, your customer may tell you they do not want to use that hypervisor for any number of reasons. As an IT architect, it is up to you to find a solution within your customer's constraints.

There are some common issues for customers to want to use or avoid certain vendors. Some may be based on a bad experience. If your customer had a massive outage due to an issue with a BackFlip Sideways 3300 network switch, they may end up removing BackFlip from their environment completely, or switch to a new vendor going forward.

Another reason is the procurement process. Customers may want to stick with in house vendors due to time constraints with a certain project. For some organizations, the procurement process may be long and tedious, especially when introducing a new vendor. Many customers get around this by purchasing equipment and software from Value Added Resellers or VARs, also commonly called partners. If a customer has an established relationship with a VAR or partner, the procurement process when purchasing from them is often streamlined. On the other hand, the customer may then be bound by what a partner sells. If you select a vendor other than what the partner already sells, the partner will still have an onboarding process for that vendor which will take time, if they are even open to selling their products.

Gaining Theoretical Knowledge

Working with procurement is something that many dread. After seeing things from both sides of the house, as a customer and a vendor, I think it could be a rather fun job. The tricky part is that each customer will have similar yet different processes for procurement in general, and their own processes for onboarding new partners and vendors. I promise you, one day you will walk into a customer and see a process completely foreign to anything else you have encountered, and this is where things can get interesting.

Your whole project, from the vendors you have selected to the time lines you have committed to can be blown if you have not spoken with procurement first. That is why it is very important to ensure someone from procurement is included on kickoff meetings with customers. Many people think of procurement after the fact, which is why some procurement people seem sort of prickly when they are approached. Many procurement professionals are used to being brought in in the very last seconds, and told they need to approve something right now, **or else**. This tactic does not usually work well for anyone involved, because there are processes that must be followed within each and every organization.

Gaining Practical Knowledge

It is time to talk about our friend the RFP once again. RFPs are very different from the customer and vendor positions, but they are a fantastic learning tool, and can often teach you a lot about many areas of an organization's business. There are often procurement timelines stated in an RFP. If customers are expecting the vendor hunger games, they are often kind enough to throw the vendors a bone, and tell them a little bit about the procurement process, and the time frame a decision is expected.

Procurement usually has a big part in an RFP. In most cases, vendors are required to send a copy of their response to procurement, as well as the technology department requesting it. In some cases, vendors respond to procurement only, and the procurement team has an internal process for review by the technology teams.

Public Presenting and Speaking

I am a little odd in the sense that I never really had any qualms about public speaking. I was asked to give a speech at a school board meeting in 7th grade by some of my teachers, and well, I just did it. I also participated in musical theater and choir in college, so I just got on stage and did that too. Now, it is not to say I do not ever get nervous. Even though I am not afraid to speak in public, I do still get the jitters at time, just like everyone else. The most nerve wracking speaking event to date I participated in was my VCDX defense. That was much harder than speaking to even a room full of people, or even a C-Level executive, both of which I have done too many times to count.

Just because I have done a lot of speaking does not mean the way I have done it has not evolved. A speaking style is something you will develop over time. You will figure out what works and what does not work for you, and you even may develop several different styles depending on the audience you are speaking to. While it is very helpful to get the feedback of others, at the end of the day, you are the one talking to the audience.

Gaining Theoretical Knowledge

Whenever you are watching someone give a talk, whether it be in person or on YouTube, think about what you do and do not like about the way they are delivering their content. If you go to enough conferences, or watch enough conference sessions, you will immediately know the type of speaker which will engage you, and the type that will bore you in the first five minutes. The key to developing your style is lots of observation, as well as trial and error on your part.

I highly recommend seeing if there is a Toastmasters club around you. Toastmasters is an international organization focusing on developing public speaking and leadership skills. Many companies will have their own clubs which will meet over lunch, so you will even be able to investigate some of these skills with your colleagues. A big part of Toastmasters is speaking in front of your club, so this will also help you gain practical knowledge.

Gaining Practical Knowledge

The best way to gain public speaking skills is to do it. There are many, many opportunities for you to do this around you. Start with your team at work. If you speak to your manager, I am sure they will be more than happy to give you some time at a staff meeting to give a brief presentation to your team on something they may find interesting. If you like your team at work this is a good starting point. If you do not like your team, this is still a good first starting point, since you will not always get to speak to friendly crowds.

Next, is your local technology user group. Chances are, whatever technology you work with today has a user group which meets not so far from you. Find out about the group, and start attending meetings. Most user groups are specifically looking for members to present during meetings.

Want to tie this into learning a technology skill? Start going to a user group meeting of a technology you are looking to learn. You will meet lots of friendly people who already know what you want to. Once you have learned enough to be dangerous, volunteer to give a talk on how the technology you are learning relates to a technology you are well versed in.

Written Communication

I have saved my absolute favorite architecture building block for last: written communication skills. For as long as I can remember, I have always loved to write (and read). I do, however, realize not everyone will share this love with me. I want to start by getting one myth I hear over and over out of the way. This myth is **engineers can't write**. If I had a dollar for every time I have heard someone say this I would probably be writing this right now (as an engineer by the way) from my own personal island.

I bring this up, because I have encountered many people of the technical persuasion who say they can't write simply because they have listened to too many people who have told them they cannot do it. Hearing this repeatedly makes people not even want to try, and that is very, very sad.

Now that we have gotten that out of the way, and you know you can indeed write, let's talk a bit more on how you can build up this very crucial skill. Writing is like a muscle. Do you think you can get off the couch today and run a marathon today? Of course not. That is why you hear all about programs like Couch to 5k which ease people into running. Writing is exactly the same, it is like a muscle you need to exercise to improve your strength.

Gaining Theoretical Knowledge

The best thing you can do to improve your writing with the least effort is to read. Read often, and read everything, not just technical resources. Make sure you pick up a good fiction book occasionally too. I have recently realized how much of my reading has been technical in nature over the last several months, and how very different technical writing can be from some fiction styles. The goal is to be exposed to many writing styles, and to begin to develop your own. I feel like I have almost been doing myself a disservice by not reading a wide enough variety of material.

Reading will also help refresh those grammar lessons you have not had in years. I could go on and on about different resources on how to communicate effectively, but first, I want you to enjoy communicating by writing before we dive into any of that.

Your goal as an IT architect is to communicate your thoughts in a clear and effective manner. This may also vary based on the audience you are talking to. You may have a customer tell you they do not want your proposals filled with all that **marketing stuff**. I know I have. You may have another customer tell you they do not want your material to be **too technical**. I have encountered this as well. The more you build your writing muscle, the easier it will become for you to be able to tailor your communication to the correct audience.

Gaining Practical Knowledge

The best way once again to gain practical knowledge in writing is to write words, lots of words. Just like I encouraged you to read all different types of materials, I also encourage you to write different types of materials.

We have talked about blogging as a great way to improve all sorts of skills, like writing and technical skills. You do not have to blog about anything technical if you do not want to, and you do not have to even have make your blogging public. However, the format of blogging is a great way to get you started with something light weight, and easy it is to achieve.

Another great way to improve your writing skills is to find writing prompts and conduct writing sprints. You would be amazed how much you can write when you get on a roll. Sometimes, I find myself writing well over 1,000 words an hour. There are many websites and Twitter accounts that post these on a regular basis, I will list some of my favorites in the Resources Appendix for you.

These are great ways to get the writing muscles going, but as I said, these are sprints, or a casual stroll. We need to work you up to the marathon that are the documentation deliverables of an IT architecture engagement. I have a couple of ideas for you on this too.

One of my personal favorites, which is NaNoWriMo, which is National Novel Writing Month. Every November people all over the world attempt to write a novel, or 50,000 words in 30 days. I have done this on numerous occasions, and I absolutely love it. The first novel I wrote for NaNoWriMo may not be fit for public consumption, but it helped me grow in leaps and bounds as a writer. If this is too ambitious for you, I along with the rest of the Virtual Design Master Creative Team run something called #vDM30in30, which is writing 30 blogs in 30 days.

Every year, we also get multiple negative comments for running this. As we know, people on the Internet are not very nice at times, and this challenge seems to bring out some real negativity. Some out there prefer to attack our platform saying our bloggers are not creating quality content, they are just trying to get something out every day. This of course, is the point. The point is to stick to a consistent writing schedule daily, and watch yourself grow as a writer. No one forces anyone to read anything on the Internet, so do not let what people say discourage you from writing, no matter what.

Writing a novel or a blog is a little different than writing a set of IT architectural deliverables, and it can be hard to get that experience. You did not think I was going to leave you hanging, did you? In this book, you will find an appendix called Your First Architecture. Here, I am going to give you a scenario to use during your journey. The goal of this scenario is giving you a platform for putting some of these skills we have been talking about into play. I will also give you some worksheets in that appendix to guide you through the process.

Becoming a Virtual Design Master

If you have gone through the Your First Architecture Appendix, and are still looking for more practice, I have something perfect for you. Several years ago, I was part of a team which created a little something called the Virtual Design Master competition. It was a crazy idea that has lasted for multiple seasons at this point. The premise is simple, it is an infrastructure design challenge with a basis in virtualization. While we started out in the early years focusing on VMware technologies, we have grown and grown as technology evolved. In the past, we have started with paper-based design scenarios which are judged by IT architects, and we also have some hands-on challenges as the season progresses. We do like to keep things interesting and keep our contestants on their toes, so we like to change the order of things sometimes.

What is even better is our challenges and solutions for every season are located at VirtualDesignMaster.io, so there are many practice scenarios just waiting for you there. You can also look at the work of the contestants to see how they may have thought of things differently, or in a similar manner to you. You can also find the videos where the contestants had to defend their design live in front of judges on the website, which are always fun to watch if you are not the one sweating in the challengers' seat.

If that was not enough, there is also a great story line to keep you occupied, full of zombies and space travel. Make sure to take a look so you can gain more IT architecture experience and have a great time doing it. I would be remiss if I did not tell you that yours truly is responsible for the creation of the scenarios for the challenges. You can either thank me or curse me after you have gotten some under your belt.

The Virtual Design Master competition is held every year, usually between June and August. Be sure to check out the website to find out when the next competition is starting, we would love to have you as a competitor.

On Our Way

Our discussion on writing reminds me of another point. You are bound to run into some negativity along the way. Someone out there will say **you cannot do it**. I am here to tell you that is a lie, and anyone reading this book can in fact, do it. What is it you ask? It could be anything. Becoming an IT architect, publishing a book, obtaining a certification like VCDX, or starting a blog. There is nothing you cannot do, as long as you are willing to put in the hard work.

Sometimes, you may not be able to get away from the person who says **you cannot do it**. The trick is to surround yourself with even more people who say **you can do it**. Surround yourself by people willing to work as hard as you are to achieve your dreams, and it will offset the unfortunate incidents when you are faced with those who are so full of negativity, they feel the need to project it onto you.

There Is More Than One Way to Build It

There is more than one way to put together the architectural building blocks, and each way will result in a different structure. It does not matter how you put the blocks together to build it, it just matters you build it. Everyone's journey will be somewhat different based on many things, such as their own unique skillset, and the time they have to devote to the journey. There is no single correct way to become an IT architect.

PART III
YOU'RE ALMOST THERE

CHAPTER 10

CERTIFICATIONS AND CONTINUED LEARNING

"You should run your life not by the calendar but how you feel, and what your interests are and ambitions."
— John Glenn

If you stand before a building, you can discover quite a bit about it before ever stepping in it. By the aesthetics, you can get a good idea of when the building was created. Buildings built in the 1930's look nothing like a building being constructed today. This is for many reasons. While materials and processes change, so do the architects constructing them. Architects are constantly researching how past buildings were designed, and changing designs for the future. The world of IT architecture as you may already know, is constantly evolving, and constantly changing. It can be a challenge for even experienced IT architects to keep up with.

Another Path to Choose From

The journey is different for everyone. You may find yourself stopping and starting your journey, or taking a path less travelled for several reasons. No matter if you pause or take a brush covered path, you will be learning something in some capacity. A big part of the journey is learning, as I am sure you have already figured out. The learning methods you have discovered so far on your IT architecture journey and the journey of life will serve you in the future.

In IT architecture, learning never stops. Think of Moore's law, from the early days of computing. Moore's law originally predicted the number of transistors in a microprocessor every two years. If we think of this from purely a microprocessor perspective, we are talking about vast increases in computing power every two years, not even accounting for new instruction sets the microprocessor is capable of.

This directly contributes to how quickly technology evolves, including our infrastructure areas of expertise. In the IT architecture world, it is especially important to keep abreast of what is going on in the technology world, which often leads us to learning new things.

Your Grown-Up Math and Spelling Test

Certifications and learning go hand in hand, and they have for quite a long time. I vividly remember the multiplication and division tests I had to take over and over and over again in second grade. These tests were called Holey Cards. They were cards with little holes in them, and you slipped a piece of paper behind the card. The teacher would set a timer, and you had until the timer ran out to answer all the questions correctly. Once you answered all of them right, you did not have to take the test anymore.

We have been tested since we entered school as children. Whether we like it or not, tests are regarded as a measure of learning. Have I ever mentioned how much I hated tests? In fourth grade, if you got the spelling test right on Monday, you did not have to take it again on Friday. Can you guess who would study on Sunday night so I did not have to take the test twice?

Certifications are no more than the grown-up version of things like math and spelling tests. Certifications are not unique to the IT industry at all, you can find them almost everywhere. Almost every vendor under the sun has at least some level of certification out there.

Levels of Certification

While each certification authority does it differently (remember, there are more than just vendor based certifications out there), we can generally group them into three major groups:

- Beginner Level
- Advanced Level
- Expert Level

Let's dive deeper into what you can expect encounter with some of these different levels of certification.

Beginner Level

This is where it all starts. You may also see these certifications referred to as associate level certifications. The beginner level certification is often a prerequisite for higher level ones, so we cannot get away from them. These generally consist of multiple choice questions over a shorter time period, such as 90 minutes or two hours. When people say certifications are a joke, these are usually the ones they are talking about.

One of the big arguments I always hear about certifications is they do not prove you know anything. With many of the beginner certifications, I completely agree. There are too many ways to cheat, which I will not even bother talking about. Multiple choice questions can also be tricky. When the tests are written, there are people sitting in a room trying to figure out how evil they can be to the test takers, and how they can confuse people. These certifications also do not often reflect on your practical knowledge on the subject matter.

Many beginner tests boil down to reading a book or two, studying some, and taking the test. There is not much more to say about a beginner level certification other than it is a necessary evil, especially if your employer requires you to take one.

Advanced Level

This is where things start to get interesting. Advanced level certifications start testing more practical knowledge. The questions are also more situational, and require much more thinking. If a beginner level certification test asks you how many virtual machines you can run on a single SuperUtraExa hypervisor host, the advanced level certification would ask about potential issues when you near that number and how to mitigate them.

Another common component of advanced certifications can be a lab component. As part of the exam, you will connect to a lab from your testing center, and deal not only with possibly horrible latency, but with the possibility of breaking your lab setup and failing the test during it. Once you get into the more advanced level certifications, you cannot really beat the system. The best thing you can do is know your stuff going into either a theoretical question based advanced certification test, or a practical lab based certification test.

Expert Level

Expert level certifications are something completely different. In many cases, they do not resemble much of the academic testing you were used to in your life. Some expert level certifications require interaction with other experts. Others simply take the advanced certification test methods to the next level. The expert level certification a journey in itself. It is not something you can study for in a weekend then pass.

There is no beating the system when it comes to the expert level certifications. Either you can perform at the expert level, or you need to focus more on your skills to get there. I find it hard believe when people bring the **certifications do not mean anything** argument to the expert level because of this. If nothing else, obtaining an expert level certification says a lot about an individual. It says they are driven and dedicated, and willing to invest their most precious resource to learn the subject matter tested: time.

Do Certifications Really Matter?

Time to break out the classic answer to every IT architecture question ever: **it depends**. I have heard people responsible for hiring say they do not care about certifications at all, but I have heard others say they value them, and if all else was equal, they would hire the person with the certification. I have also heard other say a certification may get a resume a second look versus one without. It all depends on the role, and who is doing the hiring. Some roles out there will flat out require a certain certification, especially at a partner organization.

Certifications are not the golden ticket, at all. I do believe, however, they can be a great learning tool, which I have mentioned previously. I have a couple of pieces of advice for those on the fence about following a certification path. First of all, see if your employer will pay for tests, training, or materials. Often there is a training budget, and if it does not get used, it gets lost. This is also one of those budgets that can often end up on the chopping block, so you may be doing your manager a favor by asking to use some. They might not get as big of a budget next year if they did not use it this year. If you can get the certification paid for, it really is a no brainer. Go do it. You are learning about all this stuff during your IT architecture journey anyway.

Another piece of advice is do not start a certification track on something you do not like. You should not go take the BackFlip network switch beginner certification test if you hate networking. While you now know how important it is to have expertise in all the infrastructure areas, even if you do not like them, there is no need to torture yourself with taking a certification test on one of those topics.

Ultimately, if you stick to things you find interesting, and you can get the tests paid for, there is no real reason not to get a certification. If your employer will not pay for your certification test, it is then up to you to figure out if it is financially feasible or not. While I think you will ultimately see a return on an investment you make in certification, do not put yourself in a bad financial position to take a test. The test will be there later (although it may have been updated, which is a great opportunity to sharpen your skills anyway)

How Far to Go

As someone who recently followed the VMware certification track all the way to the top in Data Center Virtualization, I can tell you following a certification track to completion is not for the faint of heart. The VCDX certification required the VCP beginner certification, then the VCAP Design and VCAP Administration advanced certifications. The VCDX itself required a design, more documentation, an application, and finally the defense which required travel.

The VCDX is a huge undertaking in itself, not to mention all of the things which had to be done before it. It required countless hours parked in front of the computer on nights and weekends. It did not only require my dedication, but the dedication of my whole family around me to support me in this mission. There are not any words for the immense satisfaction I felt when I received my VCDX number, and the feeling is still as fresh as the day I became VCDX-236.

So, the question becomes why did I do it? Why did I put in all this time and effort? This is a question everyone will have a unique answer for. First and foremost, I did it for myself. As I told you at the beginning of this book, the VCDX was a long time coming for me, and it was finally now or never. Virtualization, more specifically VMware based virtualization has been a huge passion of mine for most of my career. Every time I tried something new and different, I ended up incorporating virtualization into it somehow. A big part of obtaining VCDX for me was to prove I was an expert in this technology I had made a career out of. Beyond the technology aspect, VCDX was a way for me to prove I had the ability to design and deliver VMware based IT infrastructure solutions.

Another reason is I like to set big goals for myself, and meet them. I really enjoy the process of learning something new, and seeing how far I have come during the process. Obtaining the VCDX certification was a great way for me to do that, and as a bonus, add value to my career. Besides meeting this huge personal goal, obtaining the VCDX allowed me to prove, once and for all, I had the skillset of an IT architect.

Why I Picked VCDX

When I set out to gain an expert level certification, I picked VCDX for a reason. First, I really enjoy working with virtualization. Virtualization is a unique technology since it depends on so many of the infrastructure areas of expertise to function correctly. Because of this, if you really want to be a **virtualization person**, you need to know enough of the other infrastructure areas of expertise to be dangerous.

You cannot be **just a virtualization person** and be successful. While the VCDX does require a core competency in the virtualization arena, specifically VMware technologies since they are the issuing body, it requires so much more than **just virtualization**. The VCDX 6 blueprint is 16 pages long. That is 16 pages of what a VCDX candidate needs to be capable of. It includes the other infrastructure areas of expertise we have learned about during the journey, there is no way you are going to pass a VCDX certification without knowing how they all relate to the environment you are designing.

Very seldom does an IT architect only touch one infrastructure area of expertise. Even if you are hired to **just architect** a network environment, we have learned on our journey there is no such thing as worrying about **just the network**. I want you to take a moment and think about what other infrastructure areas would be impacted if you were to design a network. I can think of many reasons of the top of my head, and I know you can too at this point in our journey.

I saw the VCDX as the certification I wanted to use to prove my IT architecture skills to myself. While many think the VCDX is about **just virtualization**, virtualization is just the vehicle for proving your IT architecture skills. If you read through the VCDX blueprint itself, you will see it is much, much more than **just virtualization**.

Certification Burn Out

I think certification burn out is a common thing, and a common concern among many starting along a certification path. There comes a point where the thought of taking a test just makes you shudder, and there is nothing wrong with that. Personally, I do not want to be in exam center any time soon, although I know it is inevitable. Do not burn yourself out with too many tests, unless, for some strange reason, you find taking tests relaxing.

I personally do not think they are relaxing at all. If I do decide to pursue some additional certifications, I will probably stick to one certification track at a time, instead of working on a bunch of certifications at the same time. I have found that when I try to study for multiple tests at once, it just takes me longer to take the tests since I am dividing my time. My advice is to work hard on one certification at a time before moving on to the next one. This also helps avoid some of the certification burn out.

If you have taken a bunch of tests lately, and feel like you need a break, go ahead and take one. Focus on something else for a while, whether it be part of your IT architecture journey, or one of the fun goals you set yourself.

Certifications and Continued Learning

Certifications can be a great resource for trying to figure out your next learning goals, whether you take the test ultimately or not. Reading various certification blueprints are a quick way to get exposure to some topics related to a certain technology. Does this sound interesting to me, or does it sound like I would rather have a lobotomy than read anything else on this subject? After I finished VCDX, I started looking at some network certifications. Not because I was looking to take another test, but I was looking to expand some of my horizons in the networking arena, and looking for ideas on topics to research and things to destroy in the lab.

Continued Learning on Your Journey

Once you have reached a place where you are an expert in one or several infrastructure areas of expertise, and ready to dive into something new, where should you start? At this point in the journey, I am sure you know what I am already going to say. The next path you chose to take should be one you feel passionate about, and inspires you. This may be an infrastructure area of expertise, or you may want to take an architecture building block to the next level. Remember how we ranked our skills at the beginning of the journey? It is time to rank them again, except with a different ranking system in mind.

Table 9 - Skill Inspiration Ranking

	Rank	Inspiration Level
I love it!	1	This is great, I cannot wait to learn more.
	2	This was sort of interesting.
	3	This was not horrible.
	4	I made the most of this, I am glad I am done with it.
I hate it.	5	I would rather poke out my eye with a rusty spoon than learn more about this.

If you rank something a 1, you are a huge fan. You found it very interesting, and you may have spent a bit more time on if during your IT architecture journey because it was just that cool. On the other hand, if you rank a skill as a 5, you are just happy you do not have to spend any more time on it, and you are looking forward to moving on to the next thing.

First, I want you to rank your inspiration level on the infrastructure areas of expertise.

Table 10 - Infrastructure Areas of Expertise Inspiration Ranking

Infrastructure Area	Inspiration Level Ranking
Server and Compute	1 ☐ 2 ☐ 3 ☐ 4 ☐ 5 ☐
Virtualization	1 ☐ 2 ☐ 3 ☐ 4 ☐ 5 ☐
Network	1 ☐ 2 ☐ 3 ☐ 4 ☐ 5 ☐
Storage	1 ☐ 2 ☐ 3 ☐ 4 ☐ 5 ☐
Applications	1 ☐ 2 ☐ 3 ☐ 4 ☐ 5 ☐
Backup and Recovery	1 ☐ 2 ☐ 3 ☐ 4 ☐ 5 ☐
Business Continuity and Disaster Recovery	1 ☐ 2 ☐ 3 ☐ 4 ☐ 5 ☐
Security	1 ☐ 2 ☐ 3 ☐ 4 ☐ 5 ☐
	1 ☐ 2 ☐ 3 ☐ 4 ☐ 5 ☐
	1 ☐ 2 ☐ 3 ☐ 4 ☐ 5 ☐
	1 ☐ 2 ☐ 3 ☐ 4 ☐ 5 ☐

I have also included a couple of other rows for you to write down any other technologies you may have encountered during your journey. Perhaps it was one of the technologies we mentioned briefly, or something completely different. Whatever it may be, you should feel free to pursue it, even if it is not on the list we worked on.

Similar to how you ranked your inspiration when it comes to the infrastructure areas of expertise, I want you to also think about your experiences with the architectural building blocks.

Table 11 - Architectural Building Block Inspiration Ranking

Architectural Building Block	Inspiration Level Ranking
Gathering Requirements	1☐ 2☐ 3☐ 4☐ 5☐
Determining Constraints and Assumptions	1☐ 2☐ 3☐ 4☐ 5☐
Identifying and Managing Risks	1☐ 2☐ 3☐ 4☐ 5☐
Project Planning	1☐ 2☐ 3☐ 4☐ 5☐
Procurement and Vendor Management	1☐ 2☐ 3☐ 4☐ 5☐
Public Presenting and Speaking	1☐ 2☐ 3☐ 4☐ 5☐
Written Communication	1☐ 2☐ 3☐ 4☐ 5☐
	1☐ 2☐ 3☐ 4☐ 5☐
	1☐ 2☐ 3☐ 4☐ 5☐
	1☐ 2☐ 3☐ 4☐ 5☐

Once again, I have left you several blank rows to fill in anything else you have become particularly passionate about during the journey. Perhaps you have gone deeper into one of these areas, and would like to work on a specific section of an architectural building block. This is a great place to list them out.

Once you have decided on what you want to continue learning, the rest is easy. Think about the learning methods we discussed so far, and what worked best for you. Then, you can apply these methods to the existing skills you are looking to enhance, or new skills you want to build.

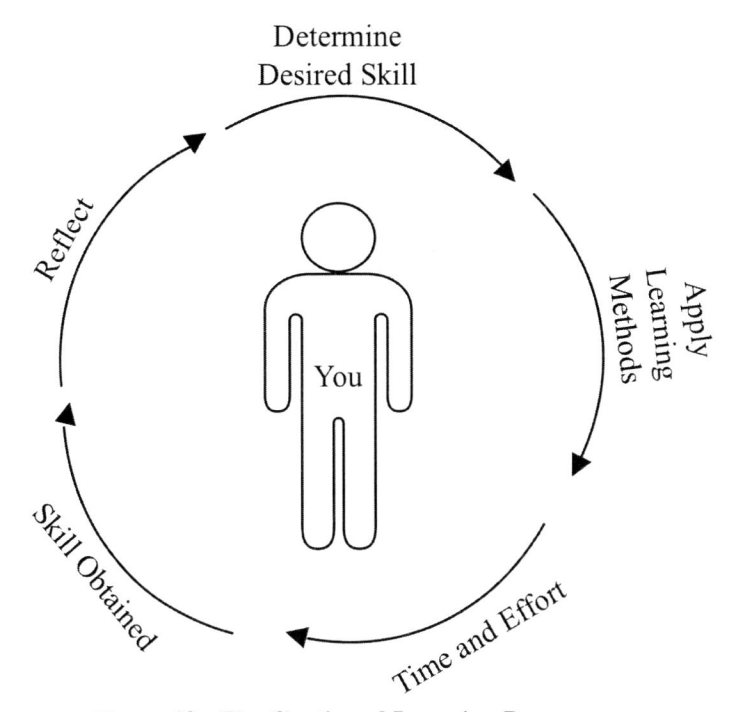

Figure 18 - The Continued Learning Process

When you have learned a new skill, always remember to reflect on the process which got you there. Ask yourself if your usual learning methods worked, or if you tried something you usually do not use. This is also a great way to get more familiar with some of the learning methods you did not use as much during the journey. Sometimes new challenges require us to think about things in a way we have not before. This is one of the reasons why it is a great idea to keep a journal of your journey. What did not work for you on one path now may work for you on a different path later.

As you continue learning during your journey, do not forget about the Resources Appendix. This appendix can help you quickly get stated learning your next new skill, whatever it may be.

You're Almost There

The lessons you have learned on your journey will serve you forever. The other day I opened my VCDX design to remind myself how and why I did something, because I was faced with a similar problem I knew I had solved before. For me, the VCDX process reinforced my architectural skills in many of the infrastructure areas of expertise, and led me to dive deeper into those areas I had not always been the biggest fan of. In just the time I wrote and defended my VCDX, I saw leaps and bounds in both my architectural and infrastructure skills. I can firmly say I am a better IT architect and better technologist after achieving the VCDX certification.

Building our skill set is key before you head down the certification path, especially if you want to take the expert level trail later. If you can find the funding and the time on your journey, certifications can be a great way to reinforce what you are doing. On the other hand, I realize certifications are not for everyone. Even if you do not elect to follow a certification path, do not discount certification material as a learning tool. The journey is full of different paths to take, and it is impossible to follow every single one. The important thing is to choose the path that will suit you best at that moment in time. If you cannot take one of the paths you would like right now, remember, paths often converge further along the trail.

CHAPTER 11

IT ARCHITECTURAL SKILLS IN PRACTICE

"All adventures, especially into new territory, are scary."
— *Sally Ride*

If we had a time machine, we could go back to ancient Egypt and ask the architect of the Great Pyramid why they designed it the way they did. Why they picked the shape, how they picked the stone, how they designed the chambers. We can ask them if they also designed the Sphinx, or if they knew the person who did. What made an architect in ancient times decide on pyramid or statue? What makes a modern architect decide to build a certain type building, be it an apartment complex, an office building, or a train station? IT architects have the same decision to make when it comes to putting their skills into practice.

IT Architecture Skills in Practice

The time has come! You have made it far enough on your journey that you want to use your newly-honed IT architecture skills daily, not just at night and on the weekends. The question you now must ask yourself is **where do you want to go from here**? You have got many options, and it all comes down to what you want to do next. If there is only one thing you learn on the journey (although I know you have learned many, many things), I hope it is **you can do anything**.

Remember at the beginning of the journey when I suggested you keep a journal? Now is a good time to read through it, and reflect on the projects you have taken part in before and during your journey so far. I am very confident you are going to see a marked difference in the way you approached things then, and the way you approach them now.

While the decision is ultimately up to you on where you want to go next, I want to give you a couple of ideas. Before I do, there is something else I want to mention

Some Really Good Advice

I have gotten the same **really good advice** from a number of people throughout my career and, guess what? It has worked every single time I have used it. The best way to get the job you want, is to go out there and do it. Wait, what? Yes, you heard me. I hope you have been using every opportunity you have been given daily to keep building your IT architecture skills in both the infrastructure areas of expertise and the architectural building blocks. You now have concrete examples of how you have put those skills to use, which can come in handy in an interview. Ever heard the phrase "If it looks like a duck, swims like a duck, and quacks like a duck, it must be a duck."? If it acts like an IT architect, and does like an IT architect, it must be an IT architect!

This advice also works if you are looking for a promotion in your current role. Almost every company has some sort of career planning guidelines. These guidelines are where the requirements for the promotion to each level are spelled out in black and white. If you have never seen this, chances are it exists someplace, and you should ask your manager for it. For some reason, some organizations offer up this information freely, and some do not. If your organization does not have these standardized guidelines, ask your manager what the requirements for the next level of your position are. From there, make sure you fulfill the requirements and document how you have done so accordingly. It is a good idea to keep a running list of these accomplishments and update them throughout the year, so you are not scrambling when review time comes.

The Next Path

Now, let's get back to trying to figure out what the next path you will take on your journey. Here are a couple of ideas to get you started on thinking about how you would like to put your IT architecture skills into practice.

Change Jobs Internally

You may work for a company you really like, and you may not want to leave. There is absolutely nothing wrong with feeling this way. If you have management supportive of what you want to do next, now is the time to take a look at the internal job postings. I cannot tell you what title you should be looking at, since each organization does things a little differently, but if you can find the word **architect** in the job description, you are probably heading in the right direction. Solutions architect and systems architect are great phrases to look for as well. With any luck, you may be able to find a very exciting position in your organization, which we're about to talk about.

The Rise of the Enterprise Architect

For a very long time, the enterprise architect was most often the person who had been at a company the longest. Usually, they were in this position because they had started as a systems analyst 20 years ago, and put most of the infrastructure into place. If your organization has someone like this, I hope you have befriended them, and more importantly, I hope they have a team reporting to them.

The enterprise architect role has been on the rise in recent years. As organizations evolve, they have begun to see the value in an individual or group performing this role. Whether an organization has an enterprise architecture role or not often depends on the maturity of the organization. Have they moved towards a centralized IT model, or are things usually done in silos? Has the organization developed standards within the realm IT infrastructure? Do they have good cross organizational communication, or is the world of IT infrastructure the wild, wild west? These are all good questions to investigate to determine if your organization would see value in the role of the enterprise architect.

Think of enterprise architects as the overseers. In many cases, IT projects must either be approved by the enterprise architecture team, or have a member from the enterprise architecture team participating in the project. The goal of the enterprise architect is to ensure a sound methodology is being followed during these IT infrastructure related projects, and to ensure all the necessary infrastructure areas of expertise are being accounted for. For example, if the storage team is looking to purchase a storage array and use an IP based storage protocol like NFS, they really should be consulting the network team to ensure the network has sufficient capacity and performance to support this new storage array and its workloads. While this makes complete sense to us at this point in our IT architecture journeys, for many it would not. You would be surprised at the number of times equipment is purchased with no regard for how it will be implemented, or how it will impact the rest of the IT infrastructure. On the other hand, if you have seen this lack of communication between groups as much as I have, you probably are not surprised at all.

Take the Other Path

In this case, the **other path** is leaving your current employer. Changing jobs in any case is no easy feat, but it can be even more nerve-wracking when you are changing employers as well. There are a couple of different ways to handle this. First, you can pick the job you want, and then pick an employer from there. On the other hand, you can target specific employers you are interested in, then look for a job suiting your IT architecture skills at those employers.

Before switching employers, make sure to pay special attention to your current employer, and the benefits they provide. How much do these benefits cost you? Does your employer contribute to a retirement account, and how much do they contribute? Is the account vested, or will you be losing something? What about stock rewards? Are you leaving behind anything there? You should be thinking of all of this as you negotiate your salary with a new company. Also, it is important to think about if the new job result in increased or decreased commuting costs?

While happiness is, of course, priceless, make sure you have a good handle on your financial package currently before negotiations on the new job begin. I cannot think of anyone who wants to change employers to make less money, and you should not want to either. This will also highly depend on the job market in your area. If the market is slow, now may not be the time to make a move, even if you really want to put those IT architecture skills into practice.

When it comes time to start climbing the hill known as a job search, do not forget to use your personal network. If you have friends or former co-workers at a company you see a job opening at, do not be shy about reaching out to them. Someone you know could be waiting for your call at that exact moment. You may be a perfect fit for an opportunity they have available. Many times, companies offer incentive programs for employees to help recruit new talent, so your friend may even be well compensated for bringing you on board. Remember, it never hurts to ask someone for their help. The worst that can happen is they say no.

Now, let's take a look at the other paths you can follow.

The Customer Path

When we think about the customer path, the roles we discussed above are certainly applicable in a customer situation. You want to be looking for enterprise architecture roles, or architecture roles in one of your infrastructure area of expertise. Do not forget to read job descriptions. The title may not have the word **architect** in it, but the job description may. The customer IT architect role can be a good spot for anyone, regardless of what you are doing today. As mentioned previously, always make sure to do your homework on the company you are interviewing with. This advice also goes beyond their compensation offerings.

You should also have a good understanding of what the company does, and what their industry is. If they are publicly traded, make sure to do some homework on how their stock ticker has been performing lately. Remember, the interview is also time to find out about the company, and your prospective coworkers, as well as their current IT infrastructure environment. Do not be shy, and make sure to ask some questions of your interviewers as well.

The Partner Path

The partner path can be an exciting path to embark on, and it is very, very different from the customer path. As a partner, you will be responsible for architecting solutions for your customer base. You will also be responsible for architecting solutions using vendors with whom the partner has established relationships. That does not mean, of course, you will not be able to start a new vendor relationship at a partner, but like most things in IT, **it depends**. Some partners have specific vendor specialties, which they use as their differentiator. For example, exclusively selling the SuperUltraExa hypervisor, and promoting themselves as SuperUltraExa experts.

Many different partners have different specializations. A partner architect role may be a good fit for you if you are passionate about the whole IT infrastructure solution stack, and can find a partner aligned with it. Unless you select something completely out of left field, it will not be too difficult to find a partner with the focus you desire. Other partners may specialize in an infrastructure area of expertise, so if you want to focus your IT architecture skills on one or two areas, a partner can also be a good place to do that.

Before we talk about partner roles, let's look at one more path you may choose to take, as the roles will be very similar.

The Vendor Path

The vendor path is also an excellent choice for the next step on your journey. The vendor path is very different from the customer path, and similar to the partner path. As a vendor, you will be responsible for architecting solutions for your customer base, using the technologies sold by your company. One of the most common phrases you will hear in the vendor space, is **sell what is on the truck**. This can also apply to certain partner environments. As a vendor, it is your job as an IT architect to be creative and ensure your technology is the one which best meets your customer's requirements.

Thinking about where your passions are will help you pick a vendor or group of vendors to take a closer look at. Some vendors may also have large professional services organizations, which can touch multiple areas instead of just the vendor's specific infrastructure area of expertise. This can be a good choice for those out there who do not want to be what they perceive as **pigeon holed**, or locked into a narrow role. Personally, I do not believe you can be pigeon holed without your consent. Each job you take is what you make of it, you will seldom be scolded for going above and beyond your job role. When I was working primarily with one technology, I certainly did not let the rest of my skillset beyond the role lapse when I held the role. I saw everything around me as an opportunity to learn something new, or to keep my skills sharp, even when they were not directly related to my day job. It is also important to remember you are not committed to a job forever. If you do feel yourself being backed into a corner for some reason, there is nothing wrong with biding your time until you can find a new place to use your skills.

Now, let's take a look at some roles within partners and vendors you may be interested in.

Don't Judge a Book by Its Cover

As I have mentioned, different companies call their roles completely different things. Two of the common ones you will encounter on the partner or the vendor side are the Systems Engineer and Solutions Architect roles. People can get into some pretty nasty fights over the different roles, and what they are supposed to do. I have also seen them used interchangeably and, in most cases, they are. Other times they are not, which just makes this whole thing more confusing.

Before you get out of your pitchforks, at one point I had the job title of Systems Engineer. Had my title been Solutions Architect, I would not have done my job any differently. As a Systems Engineer, which you will commonly see abbreviated as SE, my job was to provide solutions to my customers, which many times required me to architect them. I had to take my customer's requirements, ensure I understood the bottom line business driving them, and turn them into a solution. At times, I ended up going beyond the realm of what I was there to do, simply because it needed to be done for my customer to be successful.

Lately I have noticed the title of Solutions Architect (also known as SA) has been on the rise, probably due to the prestige of using the word architect, over the use of the title SE. There are some other cases, however, however, vendors or partners do use distinct SE and SA roles within the same organization, which brings me to my next point.

Generalists and Specialists

Believe it or not, there are different types of SEs and SAs inside a partner or vendor. At the front line, we have the generalists. These individuals know a little bit about every product sold by their company. This is enough knowledge for them to have high level and intermediate level discussions. Many times, if the company is known for one product line, they will be experts on this product.

Then come the specialists. They know fewer things, but know them very well and are able to have deep technical discussions on them. For example, if I am the BackFlip network switch company, my generalist will know the BackFlip Switch line very well. If my generalist is working with a customer who uses the SuperUltraExa hypervisor, they may elect to call in a SuperUltraExa hypervisor specialist. The specialist will help educate the customer on the value of using BackFlip network switches specifically with the SuperUltraExa hypervisor. In some cases, vendors or partners my call the generalist a SE and the specialist a SA, or an overlay SE or consulting SE. It is different everywhere, which is why it is so important to read those job descriptions during your job search so you can understand exactly what is expected of you, regardless of the title assigned.

There is also another type of SA out there, and this is the type vendors and partners bring out on a very strategic basis. This is the SA that usually has been around for quite some time and specializes in C-level messaging and presentations. Some of these SAs are no longer extremely technical, and they may rely on their fellow specialist and generalist SAs to do most of the architecture work, but these SAs are brought in to seal the deal.

If we look at some of the different options for IT architecture skills, we can visualize them as follows.

IT Architect Series: The Journey

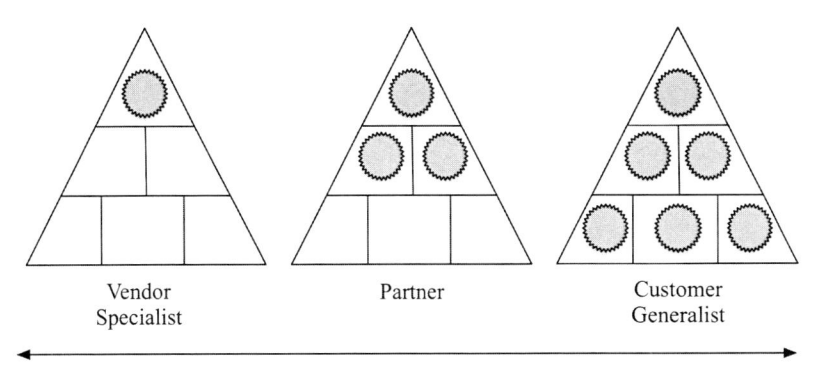

Figure 19 - Technology Opportunities

Vendor Specialist • Partner • Customer Generalist

Whether you want to be a generalist or specialist will likely depend on your personality. Some people love to know a little bit about everything, and others find it extremely frustrating and want to be an expert on something. A generalist role at a partner may be much wider than a generalist role at a vendor, just because a partner sells a wider variety of products than a vendor does. As neve wracking as it can be to change jobs, there is nothing wrong with getting experience in a generalist role, then moving to a specialist role later, or vice versa. Each type of role will give you a unique understanding of customers, their requirements, and their environments, which is priceless.

It is important to realize any role you take is what you make of it. I can try to make some generalizations about SEs and SAs but at the end of the day, it comes down to the person performing the role. Some are more hands-on than others, while some prefer to remain more theoretical. These roles are yours to craft as you see fit, as long as you are putting your customers' success first. One of the thing you will learn as you practice IT architecture is there is an exception to almost every rule. Finding the right place to put your skills into use is no exception.

If you are interested in a company, once again, leverage your network. See if someone you know is willing to give you the inside scoop on how the company structures things. A big part of the job search is finding the job and company which are right for you, and this process can take some time. Do not get discouraged if you strike out at first. It simply was not the right place for you and you will find something even better when everything is said and done.

Evaluating Which Path to Take

If you decide to take the partner or vendor path, I have some advice for you, from what I have gone through in my transition from customer to vendor. While I have never worked for a partner, I have worked with plenty of different partners, and seen many of their inner workings.

My first piece of advice is to work for a vendor or partner which sells something you are passionate about. If you despise networking, do not go work for a network vendor! Working with something you are passionate about is a big plus for many reasons. First and foremost, your customers will see your enthusiasm and passion, and they will be excited too. Secondly, you will be using that vendor's products exclusively. If you are working with them day in and day out, you had better at least like them! Another reason to stick with what excites you is who wants to go to work and be bored and miserable every day? I know I do not, and I am sure you do not either.

Another piece of advice is listen to your instincts. If something someone says during the interview process sets off alarm bells in your head, or gives you a sick feeling in your stomach, listen to yourself. No amount of money they could throw at you is worth compromising your integrity, or your beliefs. I have been very fortunate that I have never been in this situation, but I know people who have, and it was a horrible experience for them.

Finally, be yourself, and find your own way. While it will be helpful to learn from your fellow SEs or SAs when you begin your new role, make sure to find your way at the same time. My favorite thing to do as a new SE was to ask two or three people the same question. Most times, I would get two or three different answers, which would help guide me in my own direction when making a decision. The hardest part of acclimating to a new role at a partner or a vendor will probably be learning all the internal processes and systems. Learning new technology will be a breeze at this point to you in your journey. In my experience, it is not the technology but the softer things around it which take us a bit more time. When you are first beginning to put your IT architecture skills into practice, do not sign up to be the smartest person in the room. Having someone to look to for guidance in support as you begin this part of your journey is immensely valuable. In time, further along in the journey, you will return the favor to an IT architect who is just getting started.

You're Almost There

You have come a long way on your journey when you are ready to put your IT architecture skills into practice. The big decision for you now is what path to take next, when we do not know what they lead to. Will there be rocky terrain? Will it be a smooth, leisurely walk? Or are you headed up a mountain? There are times in life where we all end up on the mountain path, whether we like it or not. The path of the IT architect is no different.

Whatever the path, do not give up. I once found myself unhappy on my career path at that time. I was so unhappy, I was considering just completely jumping off the path I was on altogether, and starting over. At that point, I received some excellent advice. I was told to try one more job, perhaps two if the first did not work out. As I mentioned before, it is important to remember not every job you step into will be ideal for you. At that point, after two more tries, if I was still unhappy on the path, yes, I should absolutely jump off and do something else.

This tuned out to be some fantastic advice. I stayed on the path, my next job was fantastic, and provided me many great opportunities. It was just the thing I needed to continue my journey, completely invigorated.

See it through, because you never know what may be on the other side.

CHAPTER 12

THE DISTANCE TRAVELLED

> *"Let the future tell the truth, and evaluate each one according to his work and accomplishments. The present is theirs; the future, for which I have really worked, is mine."*
> -Nikola Tesla

The skyscrapers of today look nothing like the Great Pyramids of long ago. Similar to how architecture has evolved over time, your skills as an IT architect have evolved over the course of your journey. Whether you have chosen to validate your IT architecture skills to yourself through a certification, job change, or just incorporating them into your daily practice, you are not the same person you were when you started. You have changed.

Change Is Good

Change is a huge force in daily life, and something we will always be faced with. There are two different types of change: those we invoke, and those we run into without our consent. Through the course of your journey, you have invoked change in your skills as an IT architect, and in your day-to-day life. If you have not caught yourself using the same methodology you use when you create a new infrastructure design when you make a decision in your daily life, you will soon. You will begin to see every day problems in terms of requirements, constraints, assumptions, and risks, and make life choices accordingly.

You may not believe me right now, but applying the same methodology use for IT architecture problems to other problems will often result in a streamlined decision process. You will begin to do it without even realizing it. When we break any problem down to basics, it is easy to see how a uniform approach to problems can benefit us. I am not saying you should write a three hundred page document on what car you want to buy, but writing out a conceptual model, then several logical and physical design choices make any problem much more manageable.

When we think about how our mindset has changed during our IT architecture journey, this change is a change we have asked for. You have worked hard to undergo this change, and for some time you will still have moments when you are in awe of how far you have come. I know I do. This is also an illustration of how powerful of a force change can be, when you invoke it for a specific reason.

There is still another type of change to worry about. The change we are speaking of now is the change made to your daily life, without it being chosen. It could be your company being purchased, or a new boss. It could be a friend or loved one moving away. It could be any number of things, and these changes are often harder to cope with, since we never asked for them.

Just like your decision to pursue IT architecture was a choice, we can also look at these unforeseen changes in a different way to make them more palatable. There is one thing you can always control in life, no matter what changes are thrown your way. You can control your attitude when you wake up every single morning.

When you are faced with these changes you did not ask for, gain control of them. Choose positivity, and choose to make the change benefit you, no matter what it is. When faced with these unforeseen changes, always choose to make the most of them. There are lessons and experience hidden in these changes for us, we just need to find them.

Time for Another Lesson

You did not think we were done learning yet, did you? I want you to spend some more time reflecting on your journey, and how far you have come. You have learned all about the infrastructure areas of expertise, and you have learned about the architectural building blocks. Now, I want you to think about what you have learned about yourself.

As we change, it is important to take a good look at what we have learned during the process. Did you find new methods of learning which worked well for you? Think about how you can apply these learning methods to different areas of your life. Think about technologies you felt passionate about, and the ones you did not really like. Do you still not like these technologies or soft skills, or have you changed?

During the journey, you have also spent a lot of time with, well, yourself. Chances are you have learned a thing or two about yourself recently. I want you to really focus on these things, and see how they can evolve. Perhaps one of the things you learned well was to manage your time. This is a great lesson, and it can apply everywhere in your life. Unfortunately, not all lessons we learn are good ones. You may have developed some bad habits, like drinking too much coffee and not enough water. It is important to take a good look at all the lessons you have learned, for better or for worse.

The Most Important Lesson

It is hard to think of a single lesson as the most important one during the course of my journey. The obvious answer is the most important lesson we all learn is how to be an IT architect! We also know from the world of technology; the most obvious answer is not always the right one.

There will be times on this journey you will be full of doubt. You will be asking yourself questions like "Why am I doing this?" or even "Can I really do this?". This will happen many times. Some things that bring on this sort of crisis during the journey is struggling with a concept, or dealing with someone negative. As we discussed earlier, there will always be the person who will say, either to your face or behind your back that you cannot do something.

One lesson you have learned so far is to believe in yourself. If you did not believe you could become an IT architect, you would have never picked up this book in the first place. We all must start someplace in our journey, and it can be something as simple as writing it down as a goal, or picking up a book like this.

You may be reading this book for the first time, or you may be reading it over again later on your journey. Whatever the case, know you can do it. It may take longer than you think it will, and life may get in the way, but if you really want to be an IT architect, there is nothing standing in your way.

This goes beyond IT architecture. There is a reason I put a space for revisions in our goal sheets. Revising a goal does not mean it will not happen, and it does not mean you are giving up. It means you have the confidence in your abilities, and in yourself to do what is right, when it is right. Keep believing in yourself, and you will reach your goals, no matter what path you end up taking. This is the most important lesson we have learned during the journey.

The Art of Infrastructure Design

The first book in the IT Architect Series, *Foundation in the Art of Infrastructure Design* sums a lot up with just its title. The more you use your IT architecture skills, the more you will realize they are more of an art than a science, and continually evolve beyond learning new skills and becoming more proficient with those you already have.

Remember the two host VMware ESX design I started my journey all those years ago with? We talked about how much I have evolved as an IT architect since then, about how much I have learned about the infrastructure areas of expertise, and architectural building blocks. What we have not talked much about yet is my personal art of infrastructure design.

As part of your journey, you will find the areas you are most passionate about. This passion may come from your pure interest in a subject, or it may come from your experience. The areas with the most passion may become your art.

The art of infrastructure design is your personal calling card. These are the areas you will leave your mark on, as an IT architect in every environment you touch. Your art is what distinguishes you from other IT architects. It is different for each and every one of us, and may even change and evolve over time.

For me, I leave art in a few different areas when I touch an IT infrastructure. My first art is documentation. My passion for this comes from seeing a lot of bad documentation over the course of my career. I always want to make sure I present the customer with documentation which is clear and easy to understand. I also want them to feel good reading it, and for them to understand how much time and effort I put into it. I never want a customer to feel like I handed them something canned they could have gotten from anyone. I also like to leave personal touches throughout, to show them I am paying attention to their corporate cultures and values. Something small like using their corporate colors to annotate diagrams or slides can go a long way.

The other passion I have is to make my customers' lives easier once they implement the solution I have architected for them. I have been **thrown off the deep end** into huge complex environments, and it was not fun. I want to make sure they have a solid understanding of how to do things like operate their environment, or scaling their environment in the future. In an ideal world, by the time a project goes live with a new technology in it, a customer feels like they have been working with it for a very long time.

You will develop your own art of infrastructure design over time. To me, this is one of the most fun parts of being an IT architect. Beyond focusing on your passions, another idea is to focus on your customer's perspective. What could you do for them which would set you apart as an IT architect? This answer may be different for every customer, but you may find yourself working with many similar customers through the course of your career, so this work will not be done in vain. Inspiration on how to develop our artistic IT architecture style is all around us. We just need to be paying attention to our surroundings, like any IT architect would.

We Are All Swimmers

For some reason, idioms having do with swimming tend to be popular when it comes to change. **Sink or swim** and being **thrown of the deep end** are two of the most popular ones. I can think of a few times I have had the option of sinking or swimming, after I have been thrown off the deep end in my career.

I think one of the reasons these phrases are so popular has to do with the uniqueness of water. Water is essential to any living being. Without water, life will not continue, it is that simple. On the other hand, water also has the power to take lives in any number of ways.

These phrases both tie back to our discussion on change. The change we invoke can be just as scary as the change we never asked for. Asking for a change does not make it any less nerve-wracking. We, as humans, are creatures of habit, and we all know how hard it is to change a habit once have started it.

In either case, we may be faced with these water based idioms at some point during our journey. One of the situations comes to mind is starting a new job. In some cases, have looked long and hard for this new job, and we are excited to start it. We are nervous too, because let's face it, you do not really know what you have signed yourself up for until you walk in the door on your first day. On the other hand, you may be faced with a new job you never asked for. A good example of this is if your company is acquired, or even if your company is doing the acquiring. There is a good chance each and every one of us will be on one end of a merger or acquisition during our careers.

In either case, the only option is **swimming**. Sinking or drowning will not teach us anything. There are not any lessons to be learned from giving up. These types of situations can be excellent learning experiences. Learning about a new organization, and seeing the way it functions is worth treading water for a while. This sort of exposure will help you form your own options of the way things should be done, whether it be from a technical perspective or from a more processes based perspective. If after swimming or treading water for some time you learn the situation is not right for you, there is no harm in ultimately swimming to shore. You have built your endurance, and will be even more ready for the next swim.

Success Is Different for Everyone

At the beginning of the journey, I asked you to try and think about what success meant to you. Success is something personal, and each and every one of us sees it differently. In the world of an IT architect, we work to define success criteria for our projects and customers. In our own world, this is no different.

Now it is time to reflect on your vision of success. Did it evolve over the course of the journey? How can you apply its evolution to your next endeavor? How successful you will be depends on your personal version of success, and how hard you work for it.

Do not let other people's visions of success cloud yours. There will always be someone out there who does not think you are successful, or does not think your accomplishments mean anything. My best advice is to ignore these people. If you are proud of your accomplishments at the end of the day, that is all that matters. Anyone worth having in your life will also be proud of your accomplishments.

Back to the Word Architect

Building methods have evolved over years and years. If we just look at the example of building a house, things have changed from one hundred years ago. Building codes have changed since then, and construction methods have changed along with it. While plaster walls used to be popular, now drywall is more commonly used. Now, you may build a house and design a roof specifically for solar panels. Even in the span of 30 to 40 years, easily someone's career, the building of houses has changed.

As an IT architect, or **master builder**, we face the same thing. Our surroundings are constantly changing as new technologies are developed. The technologies we started out with also evolve over the course of time. Just think of my favorite example, virtualization. There is a huge number of IT architects out there who began their journey before the technology even existed. They had to grow and evolve over time, and learn this new technology, or they would have been left behind. They would not have been able to keep up with the requirements of their customers had they not learned the new technology of virtualization.

Just because we are IT architects today does not mean our work is done. It is up to us to apply our IT architecture skillset to new and evolving technologies. It is up to us to use these new things we have learned to create new and innovative solutions to for our customers. It is up to us to solve the seemingly impossible problems.

You're Almost There

The process of reflection on the journey never ends. When we gain new experiences, we tend to look back and see things differently. After all, hindsight is 20/20. You will continue to find more hidden lessons during your journey the more you reflect on it. Once you **believe in yourself**, the possibilities are endless.

Some lessons are harder than others. You may find yourself wishing you had done something differently at times during the journey. In these cases, reflection is even more important. Reflect on why you wish you had not done things the way you did, but do not obsess over it. What has been done has been done. It is up to you to learn from the experience, and do things differently in the future. We can waste a great deal of time and energy on the things we cannot change, but that is time and energy that could be put to better use focusing on the future. Life is a constant loop of reflecting, learning, and moving forward.

Now that you have proven to yourself **you can do anything**, it is time to set new goals for yourself, and decide what path to take next. This is no easy task. It also was not an easy task to become an IT architect, but you have accomplished it.

CHAPTER 13

THE NEXT CHAPTER

> *"A journey is a person in itself; no two are alike. And all plans, safeguards, policing, and coercion are fruitless. We find that after years of struggle that we do not take a trip; a trip takes us."*
> — John Steinbeck

For as long as I can remember, one of my personal goals has always been to write a book, and publish it. When I step back and think about it, I believe my love of writing evolved from my love of reading. For as long as I can remember I was always the child with their head in the book. I cannot tell you how many times I got in trouble in high school for reading a novel in class instead of paying attention. To this day, I will wait in line at midnight for books to come out, then stay up all night reading them.

An IT Architect's Biggest Secret

You may think, as you get to the end of this book, your journey to becoming an IT architect is almost over. I hope you have made notes, folded corners, and left sticky notes on the pages of this book at this point in your journey.

I hope you have gone through your journal and the Self-Assessment Appendix a few times, and seen the growth in your technical and softer skills. Perhaps you are getting ready to take on the job search for your first role as an IT architect, or you have just settled into a new job. Or maybe, you are working on a new certification path. At this point in our journey together, I think it is time for me to share the biggest secret of the IT architect with you.

The journey never ends.

Yes, you read that right. The journey never ends.

As IT architects, we all share a natural curiosity, and a love of learning, otherwise, why would we have started this journey in the first place? Why would we have spent our most precious resource working on these skills? We would not have.

Your IT architecture journey will continue to grow and evolve as new technologies emerge, and you gain more and more practical IT architecture experience. Even the most seasoned IT architects in the world continue to learn new things daily, it simply is in our DNA as an IT architect.

The Path We've Travelled

We have come a long way on our journey so far. We have talked about what an IT architect is, and the questions to ask yourself as you begin your journey. When it comes to evaluating the skills you have, honesty now will only help you later on in the journey, which is why I created the Self-Assessment Workbook for you.

Another important topic we have discussed is learning. While you may think you are a certain type of learner, it is important to explore learning methods. Discovering a new method of learning will help us on our IT architecture journey, and any other roads we travel. There are different types of knowledge to gain during the journey which can be categorized into two main types; theoretical and practical. Both types of knowledge are equally important during the course of the journey.

A big part of your IT architecture journey is learning about the technology you will need to use to build solutions for your customers. There are so many technologies to cover, many more than could ever fit in this book. I selected a core group of technologies for us to focus on I like to call the infrastructure areas of expertise:

- Server and Compute
- Virtualization and Virtual Machines
- Network
- Storage
- Applications

- Backup and Recovery
- Business Continuity and Disaster Recovery
- Security

It is important for IT architects to understand the technologies they will use, as well as how these technologies interact with each other. We talked about ways to gain both theoretical and practical knowledge of these technologies, and why they are so important.

Aspiring IT architects often overlook the softer skills they will require on their journey. These skills, which I like to call the architectural building blocks are what will be required of them as they begin to bring solutions to customers. These softer skills are:

- Gathering Requirements
- Determining Constraints
- You Know What They Say About Assumptions
- Identifying and Managing Risks
- Project Planning
- Procurement and Vendor Management
- Public Presenting and Speaking
- Written Communication

We applied our different methods of learning to these softer skills to gain theoretical and practical knowledge in them.

There is quite a bit of material to learn when becoming an IT architect, and we are all bound to run into topics we do not feel as passionate about. Nonetheless, all the skills we need to acquire are important to our journey. We talked about some strategies for working with the skills we are not as fond of, such as taking a look at why you are not a fan of the skill, and finding a lesson within the situation. If all else fails, bribing yourself does not hurt either. In my experience, it is better to get learning these topics over with earlier, rather than waiting towards the end of your journey.

As you develop your skills, you may want to head down the path of certifications, or continue your journey by learning something new. This book is more than just a guide to your IT architecture journey, the lessons in here will serve you on future journeys to come. You can apply the methods we developed for this journey to the next one.

The time will also come for you to put your IT architecture skills into practice. You may want to change jobs, and we talked about some positions and possible paths out there for you to take. If you end up on the wrong path, remember it is not permanent. While sometimes a path may be full of rough terrain, it can turn into a leisurely path with some perseverance and hard work.

The Story of Life

The biggest goal I had when I began this book was to arm you with the tools you would need during your IT architecture journey. I can tell you from experience, these tools also translate to other chapters in the story of life.

This is why I ended every chapter with some advice I learned during my own journey. Every piece of advice I have mentioned can be applied to more than just your IT architecture journey. These lessons can be applied to anything you want to accomplish, whether it be personal or professional. In writing this book, I applied many of the methods and lessons we talked about. I know what I leaned on my IT architecture journey will continue to serve me for many years to come. I hope it will continue to serve you, as well.

The Possibilities Are Endless

Over the course of your journey, you have proved to yourself you can do anything you put your mind to. This knowledge is more precious than the knowledge of any technology or soft skill you have gained so far in your journey. Now, armed with this knowledge, the possibilities are endless. Whatever you decide you want to accomplish next in life, you now have proof you can accomplish anything with hard work and perseverance.

The Next Chapter

If you still are not exactly sure what you were going to write in the next chapter of your life, or what path you are going to take next in your journey, do not worry. It is perfectly normal. Many times, after we reach a goal we have set for ourselves, we are not quite sure what to do next. You may now be a practicing IT architect, but you will soon start looking for the next chapter to write, or the next path to take.

Perhaps it is becoming an expert in a new infrastructure area of expertise, or perhaps it is exploring an architectural building block further you have found interesting. It could also be something completely unrelated to IT architecture at all. Whatever it is, you are now prepared to take it on, and be successful in it.

The Journey Continues

If you are reading this, that means we are both about to embark on the next part of our journeys. I have finally written and published a book, and you are well along on the path of becoming an IT architect. I did not call this chapter **The End** or **The Last Chapter**, I called it **The Next Chapter**.

Wherever you go next, whether it be on your IT architecture journey or simply the journey of life, I hope you are more prepared for it after our time together. I hope I have introduced you to new ways of learning and thinking that you can apply to every journey you take from here on out. A journey will not always be easy, and you may not see the immediate value or benefit of the challenges you face. Every journey, however, is worth it. Every journey you take is what you make of it. You can learn something from every step you take. Every step you take is another step in the right direction.

Thank you for taking me along with you. Enjoy the journey.

PART IV
APPENDICES

APPENDIX A
SELF-ASSESSMENT WORKBOOK

"The noblest pleasure is the joy of understanding."
— *Leonardo da Vinci*

Welcome to the Self-Assessment Workbook. This workbook serves as a starting place for you to begin the process of evaluating your current IT architecture skillset. Remember, a little bit of honesty with yourself now will go a long way in building the foundation to your success as an IT architect.

Why Am I Doing This?

When we begin our self-assessment, we must ask ourselves some very important questions. Take a moment to review these questions, and write down your answers.

Why Am I Beginning This Journey?	Date:

What Do I Want to Do?	Date:

What are some technologies I enjoy working with?	Date:
1.	
2.	
3.	
4.	
5.	

Where Do I Want to go?	Date:

Self-Assessment Guidelines

We are going to use the following ranking system to assess your skills. Remember to be honest, and do not worry, this stays between us.

	Rank	Skill Description
Low Skill	1	I can spell it.
	2	I have a vague understanding of it.
	3	I can hold a decent conversation on it.
	4	I have a good understanding of it, and feel comfortable working with it.
High Skill	5	I can teach someone how it works.

Technology Skills Self-Assessment

Now, it is time to assess our technology skills today, and decide where we want them to be in the future.

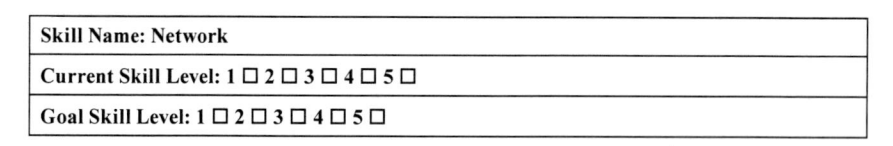

Skill Name: Server & Compute
Current Skill Level: 1 ☐ 2 ☐ 3 ☐ 4 ☐ 5 ☐
Goal Skill Level: 1 ☐ 2 ☐ 3 ☐ 4 ☐ 5 ☐

Skill Name: Virtualization
Current Skill Level: 1 ☐ 2 ☐ 3 ☐ 4 ☐ 5 ☐
Goal Skill Level: 1 ☐ 2 ☐ 3 ☐ 4 ☐ 5 ☐

Skill Name: Network
Current Skill Level: 1 ☐ 2 ☐ 3 ☐ 4 ☐ 5 ☐
Goal Skill Level: 1 ☐ 2 ☐ 3 ☐ 4 ☐ 5 ☐

Skill Name: Storage
Current Skill Level: 1 ☐ 2 ☐ 3 ☐ 4 ☐ 5 ☐
Goal Skill Level: 1 ☐ 2 ☐ 3 ☐ 4 ☐ 5 ☐

Skill Name: Applications
Current Skill Level: 1 ☐ 2 ☐ 3 ☐ 4 ☐ 5 ☐
Goal Skill Level: 1 ☐ 2 ☐ 3 ☐ 4 ☐ 5 ☐

Skill Name: Backup & Recovery
Current Skill Level: 1 ☐ 2 ☐ 3 ☐ 4 ☐ 5 ☐
Goal Skill Level: 1 ☐ 2 ☐ 3 ☐ 4 ☐ 5 ☐

Skill Name: Business Continuity/Disaster Recovery
Current Skill Level: 1 ☐ 2 ☐ 3 ☐ 4 ☐ 5 ☐
Goal Skill Level: 1 ☐ 2 ☐ 3 ☐ 4 ☐ 5 ☐

Skill Name: Security
Current Skill Level: 1 ☐ 2 ☐ 3 ☐ 4 ☐ 5 ☐
Goal Skill Level: 1 ☐ 2 ☐ 3 ☐ 4 ☐ 5 ☐

Skill Name:
Current Skill Level: 1 ☐ 2 ☐ 3 ☐ 4 ☐ 5 ☐
Goal Skill Level: 1 ☐ 2 ☐ 3 ☐ 4 ☐ 5 ☐

Skill Name:
Current Skill Level: 1 ☐ 2 ☐ 3 ☐ 4 ☐ 5 ☐
Goal Skill Level: 1 ☐ 2 ☐ 3 ☐ 4 ☐ 5 ☐

Melissa Palmer

Technology Skills Goal Sheets

Since we now know what our skills are, and where we want them to go, let's work on how we are going to get there with the following goal sheets. Have more goals? Good, I am glad! You can find more goal sheets on the *IT Architect Series* website located at http://www.itaseries.com/.

Technology Goal Sheet 1

Technology Name:		
Today's Date:	Goal Completion Date:	Time To Complete:
End Goal:		
Top 3 Things I need to work on:		
Other Things I Want to Learn:		
Issues I think I may encounter and How to overcome them:		
Revisions:		
Goal Met Actual Date:		

Technology Goal Sheet 2

Technology Name:		
Today's Date:	Goal Completion Date:	Time To Complete:
End Goal:		
Top 3 Things I need to work on:		
Other Things I Want to Learn:		
Issues I think I may encounter and How to overcome them:		
Revisions:		
Goal Met Actual Date:		

Technology Goal Sheet 3

Technology Name:		
Today's Date:	Goal Completion Date:	Time To Complete:
End Goal:		
Top 3 Things I need to work on:		
Other Things I Want to Learn:		
Issues I think I may encounter and How to overcome them:		
Revisions:		
Goal Met Actual Date:		

Soft Skills Self-Assessment

The below tables are to assess your current soft skills as they stand today, and determine where you want them to be in the future.

Skill Name: Gathering Requirements
Current Skill Level: 1 ☐ 2 ☐ 3 ☐ 4 ☐ 5 ☐
Goal Skill Level: 1 ☐ 2 ☐ 3 ☐ 4 ☐ 5 ☐

Skill Name: Determining Constraints and Assumptions
Current Skill Level: 1 ☐ 2 ☐ 3 ☐ 4 ☐ 5 ☐
Goal Skill Level: 1 ☐ 2 ☐ 3 ☐ 4 ☐ 5 ☐

Skill Name: Identifying and Managing Risks
Current Skill Level: 1 ☐ 2 ☐ 3 ☐ 4 ☐ 5 ☐
Goal Skill Level: 1 ☐ 2 ☐ 3 ☐ 4 ☐ 5 ☐

Skill Name: Project Planning
Current Skill Level: 1 ☐ 2 ☐ 3 ☐ 4 ☐ 5 ☐
Goal Skill Level: 1 ☐ 2 ☐ 3 ☐ 4 ☐ 5 ☐

Skill Name: Procurement and Vendor Management
Current Skill Level: 1 ☐ 2 ☐ 3 ☐ 4 ☐ 5 ☐
Goal Skill Level: 1 ☐ 2 ☐ 3 ☐ 4 ☐ 5 ☐

Skill Name: Public Presenting and Speaking
Current Skill Level: 1 ☐ 2 ☐ 3 ☐ 4 ☐ 5 ☐
Goal Skill Level: 1 ☐ 2 ☐ 3 ☐ 4 ☐ 5 ☐

Skill Name:
Current Skill Level: 1 ☐ 2 ☐ 3 ☐ 4 ☐ 5 ☐
Goal Skill Level: 1 ☐ 2 ☐ 3 ☐ 4 ☐ 5 ☐

Skill Name:
Current Skill Level: 1 ☐ 2 ☐ 3 ☐ 4 ☐ 5 ☐
Goal Skill Level: 1 ☐ 2 ☐ 3 ☐ 4 ☐ 5 ☐

Soft Skills Goal Sheets

Since we know what our skills are, and where we want them to go, let's work on how we are going to get there.

Soft Skills Goal Sheet 1

Skill Name:		
Today's Date:	Goal Completion Date:	Time To Complete:
End Goal:		
Top 3 Things I need to work on:		
Other Things I Want to Learn:		
Issues I think I may encounter and How to overcome them:		
Revisions:		
Goal Met Actual Date:		

Melissa Palmer

Soft Skills Goal Sheet 2

Skill Name:		
Today's Date:	Goal Completion Date:	Time To Complete:
End Goal:		
Top 3 Things I need to work on:		
Other Things I Want to Learn:		
Issues I think I may encounter and How to overcome them:		
Revisions:		
Goal Met Actual Date:		

Soft Skills Goal Sheet 3

Skill Name:		
Today's Date:	Goal Completion Date:	Time To Complete:
End Goal:		
Top 3 Things I need to work on:		
Other Things I Want to Learn:		
Issues I think I may encounter and How to overcome them:		
Revisions:		
Goal Met Actual Date:		

Fun Skill Goal Sheet

This goal sheet is meant for something fun, and not related to your IT architecture journey. It is important to keep things in perspective, and to make sure your mind is active with other things besides IT architecture.

Fun Skill Goal Sheet

Fun Skill Name:		
Today's Date:	Goal Completion Date:	Time To Complete:
End Goal:		
Top 3 Things I need to work on:		
Other Things I Want to Learn:		
Issues I think I may encounter and How to overcome them:		
Revisions:		
Goal Met Actual Date:		

Your Version of Success

We also talked about what success looks like for you. Here is a place for you to begin brainstorming what a successful IT architecture journey means to you.

Your Version of Success Sheet

When I hear the word "Success", the first three words that come to mind are...		
Word 1:	Word 2:	Word 3:
A successful journey means....		
Revisions to my idea of success...		
Today's Date:		
Revision Dates:		

Need More?

Do you have more goals to set? Do you want to use this workbook another way? No problem. This workbook, as well as goal sheets are available for the *IT Architect Series* website located at http://www.itaseries.com.

APPENDIX B

YOUR FIRST IT ARCHITECTURE

> *"Success is not final, failure is not fatal: it is the courage to continue that counts."*
> — *Winston Churchill*

This appendix consists of a scenario I have created for you to practice your IT architecture skills on. After the scenario, you will find a workbook to guide you through the process of creating your first IT architecture design. Just go for it. Do not worry about being perfect, and do not worry about the final product. This is your chance to put the skills you have been working on to use, perhaps for the first time. In this case, there are no right or wrong answers, as long as you justify them. There is no failure in this design, only success. Good luck, and have fun.

The Scenario

Thirty M Three, Inc. is an online store which specializes in high-tech kitchen gadgets for fine cooking. They have grown quite a bit in the last several years, and are looking to build a new state of the art IT infrastructure. Thirty M Three has a great relationship with their current colocation provider, and will be expanding from a single rack of dated equipment to a cage of a yet to be determined size. Thirty M Three currently has equipment on the East Coast of the United States, and is entertaining the idea of also putting equipment on the West Coast. Last year, they suffered significant losses when their website went down right before a major holiday.

The Thirty M Three staff is growing, and they are now allowing employees a budget to purchase whatever device they would like to use for their daily activities. They need an IT infrastructure for these devices to connect to in order to run office applications, as well as some of the Thirty M Three specialized software suites.

Thirty M Three currently hosts their website in their existing rack, and has been having intermittent performance problems. They do not have anything in place to handle any sort of equipment failure. Their website and e-commerce application are two of their most critical apps. They also have an application called MMM Nice which they use to track potential products and vendors they are interested in starting relationships with.

Thirty M Three does not have a budget in place for the project, but they want a cost effective yet flexible and powerful solution. Like most e-commerce providers, they are busier around holidays and need to ensure their systems are highly available with no data loss during these periods. Thirty M Three wants to leverage some existing servers that are at the end of their support contract if possible to reduce costs. The Thirty M Three storage array is no longer supported, and drives are purchased online in the event of a failure.

Thirty M Three accepts all major credit cards on their website, and also offers subscriptions for some products. They also have a very important application which tracks their inventory, which they have had many issues with in the past, since it runs on a very old server. Thirty M Three would also like to ensure they stay ahead of the curve when it comes to high-tech kitchen gadgets for fine cooking. They hired several developers who are currently working on creating various mobile apps for sharing recipes and cooking techniques. They are also trying to develop themselves as a lifestyle brand, and are very active in social media. However, their current infrastructure cannot keep up if one of their posts were to go viral.

Most of the Thirty M Three technology staff does not have much experience, so they are concerned with being able to run the environment once it has gone live, and would like to receive training on the new environment.

Thirty M Three is looking forward to working with you, and cannot wait for their new infrastructure to be designed and implemented.

Your First Architecture

You can use the following guide/sheet for creating your IT architecture design. I have included five blank spaces for each portion of the conceptual model, and two blank spaces for each design choice in the logical and physical models. I also encourage you to try and draw diagrams as part of your design. Your journal is a great place to put these diagrams, and any additional content you create as part of the design process. You can also download this scenario on the *IT Architect Series* website.

Conceptual Design

	Requirements
R1	
R2	
R3	
R4	
R5	

	Constraints
C1	
C2	
C3	
C4	
C5	

	Assumptions
A1	
A2	
A3	
A4	
A5	

	Risks
RI1	
RI2	
RI3	
RI4	
RI5	

Do not forget to mitigate these risks somewhere during the design process. If you introduce a risk as part of a design choice, be sure to mitigate it as well.

Logical Compute Design

Logical Design Choice 1	Compute
Design Choice:	
Justification:	
Impact of Choice:	
How Choice Meets Requirements:	
Other Relevant Information:	

Logical Design Choice 2	Compute
Design Choice:	
Justification:	
Impact of Choice:	
How Choice Meets Requirements:	
Other Relevant Information:	

Physical Compute Design

Physical Design Choice 1	Compute
Design Choice:	
Justification:	
Impact of Choice:	
How Choice Meets Requirements:	
Other Relevant Information:	

Physical Design Choice 2	Compute
Design Choice:	
Justification:	
Impact of Choice:	
How Choice Meets Requirements:	
Other Relevant Information:	

IT Architect Series: The Journey

Logical Virtualization Design

Logical Design Choice 1	Virtualization
Design Choice:	
Justification:	
Impact of Choice:	
How Choice Meets Requirements:	
Other Relevant Information:	

Logical Design Choice 2	Virtualization
Design Choice:	
Justification:	
Impact of Choice:	
How Choice Meets Requirements:	
Other Relevant Information:	

Physical Virtualization Design

Physical Design Choice 1	Virtualization
Design Choice:	
Justification:	
Impact of Choice:	
How Choice Meets Requirements:	
Other Relevant Information:	

Physical Design Choice 2	Virtualization
Design Choice:	
Justification:	
Impact of Choice:	
How Choice Meets Requirements:	
Other Relevant Information:	

Logical Network Design

Logical Design Choice 1	Network
Design Choice:	
Justification:	
Impact of Choice:	
How Choice Meets Requirements:	
Other Relevant Information:	

Logical Design Choice 2	Network
Design Choice:	
Justification:	
Impact of Choice:	
How Choice Meets Requirements:	
Other Relevant Information:	

Physical Network Design

Physical Design Choice 1	Network
Design Choice:	
Justification:	
Impact of Choice:	
How Choice Meets Requirements:	
Other Relevant Information:	

Physical Design Choice 2	Network
Design Choice:	
Justification:	
Impact of Choice:	
How Choice Meets Requirements:	
Other Relevant Information:	

Logical Storage Design

Logical Design Choice 1	Storage
Design Choice:	
Justification:	
Impact of Choice:	
How Choice Meets Requirements:	
Other Relevant Information:	

Logical Design Choice 2	Storage
Design Choice:	
Justification:	
Impact of Choice:	
How Choice Meets Requirements:	
Other Relevant Information:	

Physical Storage Design

Physical Design Choice 1	Storage
Design Choice:	
Justification:	
Impact of Choice:	
How Choice Meets Requirements:	
Other Relevant Information:	

Physical Design Choice 2	Storage
Design Choice:	
Justification:	
Impact of Choice:	
How Choice Meets Requirements:	
Other Relevant Information:	

Logical Application Design

Logical Design Choice 1	Application
Design Choice:	
Justification:	
Impact of Choice:	
How Choice Meets Requirements:	
Other Relevant Information:	

Logical Design Choice 2	Application
Design Choice:	
Justification:	
Impact of Choice:	
How Choice Meets Requirements:	
Other Relevant Information:	

Physical Application Design

Physical Design Choice 1	Application
Design Choice:	
Justification:	
Impact of Choice:	
How Choice Meets Requirements:	
Other Relevant Information:	

Physical Design Choice 2	Application
Design Choice:	
Justification:	
Impact of Choice:	
How Choice Meets Requirements:	
Other Relevant Information:	

Logical Backup and Recovery Design

Logical Design Choice 1	Backup and Recovery
Design Choice:	
Justification:	
Impact of Choice:	
How Choice Meets Requirements:	
Other Relevant Information:	

Logical Design Choice 2	Backup and Recovery
Design Choice:	
Justification:	
Impact of Choice:	
How Choice Meets Requirements:	
Other Relevant Information:	

Physical Backup and Recovery Design

Physical Design Choice 1	Backup and Recovery
Design Choice:	
Justification:	
Impact of Choice:	
How Choice Meets Requirements:	
Other Relevant Information:	

Physical Design Choice 2	Backup and Recovery
Design Choice:	
Justification:	
Impact of Choice:	
How Choice Meets Requirements:	
Other Relevant Information:	

Logical Business Continuity and Disaster Recovery Design

Logical Design Choice 1	Business Continuity and Disaster Recovery
Design Choice:	
Justification:	
Impact of Choice:	
How Choice Meets Requirements:	
Other Relevant Information:	

Logical Design Choice 2	Business Continuity and Disaster Recovery
Design Choice:	
Justification:	
Impact of Choice:	
How Choice Meets Requirements:	
Other Relevant Information:	

Physical Business Continuity and Disaster Recovery Design

Physical Design Choice 1	Business Continuity and Disaster Recovery
Design Choice:	
Justification:	
Impact of Choice:	
How Choice Meets Requirements:	
Other Relevant Information:	

Physical Design Choice 2	Business Continuity and Disaster Recovery
Design Choice:	
Justification:	
Impact of Choice:	
How Choice Meets Requirements:	
Other Relevant Information:	

Logical Security Design

Logical Design Choice 1	Security
Design Choice:	
Justification:	
Impact of Choice:	
How Choice Meets Requirements:	
Other Relevant Information:	

Logical Design Choice 2	Security
Design Choice:	
Justification:	
Impact of Choice:	
How Choice Meets Requirements:	
Other Relevant Information:	

Physical Security Design

Physical Design Choice 1	Security
Design Choice:	
Justification:	
Impact of Choice:	
How Choice Meets Requirements:	
Other Relevant Information:	

Physical Design Choice 2	Security
Design Choice:	
Justification:	
Impact of Choice:	
How Choice Meets Requirements:	
Other Relevant Information:	

Other Technologies

Are there other technologies beyond the infrastructure areas of expertise you wish to use to create the solution for Thirty M Three? If so, you can use this space to create the logical and physical designs for them.

Logical Design

Logical Design Choice 1	Other
Design Choice:	
Justification:	
Impact of Choice:	
How Choice Meets Requirements:	
Other Relevant Information:	

Logical Design Choice 2	Other
Design Choice:	
Justification:	
Impact of Choice:	
How Choice Meets Requirements:	
Other Relevant Information:	

Physical Design

Physical Design Choice 1	Other
Design Choice:	
Justification:	
Impact of Choice:	
How Choice Meets Requirements:	
Other Relevant Information:	

Physical Design Choice 2	Other
Design Choice:	
Justification:	
Impact of Choice:	
How Choice Meets Requirements:	
Other Relevant Information:	

Providing the Total Solution

Remember, as part of an IT architecture engagement, you need to deliver much more than just the design for your customer's environment. Think of everything which will need to be done after your design has been approved. The following documentation will also need to be created to provide your customer with a total solution.

- Implementation Plan
- Installation Guide
- Standard Operating Procedures
- Validation and Testing Plan

Now, I want you to create four blank documents, and begin your supporting documentation as listed above. For now, keep it short. Instead of writing the documents, think about what you would like to see in each one of these documents. That is what I want you to write right now. As you continue your journey, and gain more experience, your views may change. Come back to these documents, and edit them accordingly.

The Next Steps

Now that you have the beginnings of an IT architecture design, as well as an idea of what should be in the supporting documentation, I want you to step away from it for a day or two. Then, I want you to share it with someone. It could be your mentor, or it could be someone else along the journey. It could also be a friend or coworker who is willing to listen. Talking through these documents will help you get a fresh perspective on it, and it is always nice to bounce ideas off someone else. We all bring a unique perspective to an IT architecture project due to our unique experience. The experience of others is almost as invaluable as your own experience.

Congratulations!
You have created your first
IT architecture design!

APPENDIX C
RESOURCES

"Research is creating new knowledge."
— *Neil Armstrong*

The Resources Appendix is a condensed guide for the journey. There is a great deal of material in this book, so I want to make sure you have easy access to the things you will be using over and over. I have listed the resources I found helpful during the journey, and consulted other IT architects to find out their favorite resources.

Get Started with A Lab

Your lab will be essential to your journey as an IT architect. It can come in many different forms, and it may even evolve over time. Here are some ideas on getting started:

- Build a lab at work from old hardware
- Get access to other team's labs at work
- Get a good computer with at least 16 GB of RAM to get started with a lab at home, the more ram and more powerful, the better!
- Use the cloud (Which can get pricy! Always remember to turn things off when you are done if you go this route, and pay attention to what things really cost.)
- For more cost-effective options, look at the Amazon Web Services (AWS) Free Tier Offering as well as consider having your employer sponsor a Microsoft Developer Network (MSDN) subscription for the free Azure credits
- Take a look at the Open Homelab Project (https://openhomelab.org). The Open Homelab Project can guide you through many decision points for determining the best home lab for you, and creating it.

- VMware Hands-on Labs (http://labs.hol.vmware.com/) is a great resource for introduction to a number of VMware technologies. You can follow the provided lab guides, or spin up a lab and do what you wish.

Technology Learning

The following resources can be applied to learning infrastructure skills or technology skills you want to learn.

Especially for Network Skills

Network equipment is not cheap. If you cannot get access to network equipment at work, you will need to spend a little bit of money to get some hands-on practice. If you go the eBay Special route, be sure to confirm the models you are purchasing can run the software you need to practice with.

- Look for CCIE (Cisco Certified Internetwork Expert) and Cisco Certification Rack Rentals
- Look at network simulators
    - Cisco's Virtual Internet Routing Lab (VIRL)
    - GNS3

Storage Skills Are Similar

If you are looking to get hands on experience with enterprise class storage equipment, simulators are also a fantastic option. Research the availability of storage simulators based on what vendor you would like to gain hands on experience on. You can also ask your friendly neighborhood Storage Vendor SE if there is simulator software available for their product.

Vendor Materials

Vendor materials can be fantastic resource when learning a new technology. Remember to keep in mind our discussion on best practices, and think about how a specific vendor's product would integrate into the rest of the IT infrastructure.

- Spec Sheets and Technical Specifications (Vendors often have different terms for this, but this is the document which lists the specifications such as capacity, power, clock speeds, RAM, etc.)
- White Papers
- Frequently Asked Questions (FAQs)
- Technical Reports
- Technical Blogs
- Case Studies
- Free Vendor Training

Conference Sessions

Session materials from conferences are a great learning resource. Here is a list of conferences which provide their material for free to get you started. Be sure to research associated conferences for technologies you are looking to learn about.

- VMworld
- Cisco LIVE!
- OpenStack Summit
- AWS re:Invent
- Microsoft Ignite

Certification Materials

Remember to always download the blueprint or exam outline for each certification. This is your true guide to learning the material. Here are some certifications you may find helpful to building your technical skills.

- Cisco - CCNA/CCNP/CCIE
- VMware - VCP/VCAP/VCDX
- (ISC)² - CISSP
- PMI - PMP
- Microsoft - MCSE/MCSA
- Red Hat - RHCE
- AWS Certifications (Especially the AWS Certified Solution Architect track)

Free Trials and NFR Licenses

Many vendors offer free trials or NFR licenses of their software. This can be a great way to get some practical hand-on experience with a product. You may be able also to ask your SE for an evaluation license.

General Learning

Architect Your Life

You are surrounded by opportunities to hone those IT architecture skills. Create designs from random things in your life. Not sure where to go to dinner? Do not worry, that problem is a great learning opportunity.

- Come up with a conceptual design, and design choices for day to day problems you face
- Use projects at work for material to help you practice components of the conceptual design

Public Speaking Resources

Some may find public speaking to be one of the more intimidating aspects of becoming an IT architect. There are many opportunities to work on this skill such as:

- Starting with your team at work. Volunteer to give a presentation on a relevant topic during a staff meeting.
- Look for a local Toastmasters International chapter at https://www.toastmasters.org/
- Join a local technology user group (see dedicated section below)

Writing Resources

The best way to work on your writing skills is to practice, practice, practice! Beyond practicing, reading is also a great way to get better at writing.

- Start a blog to practice writing
    - Blog about anything you want, IT architecture skills you are working on are a great place to start
- Practice writing by setting a timer and picking a writing prompt.
    - Anywhere from 5 to 20 minutes is a good guide for getting started. A Google/Google Images search for "writing prompts" will give you some ideas to get started.
    - A writing prompt twitter: https://twitter.com/DailyPrompt
    - A fun website with 60 second writing prompts: http://www.oneword.com/

General Resources

Here are some general resources which do not map specifically to one type of IT architecture skill or another. These resources will help you build skills in many areas.

Your Local Community College

Taking a class at a local community college is a great way to build a skill during your IT architecture journey. You will be able to find a variety of courses focused on both technical and soft skills. Be sure to check their schedule a few times per year, as some courses may be offered at different times (for example, they may only offer Introduction to Networking in during the fall semester).

Your Coworkers

Your coworkers are a great resource, because they all know something you do not. Likewise, you know something they do not. They can be a great resource for learning the infrastructure areas of expertise, or working on some of the architecture building blocks. There are numerous ways your coworkers can help you on the journey.

- Ask a coworker to be a mentor
- Propose a knowledge exchange: you teach them, they teach you
- Simply ask a coworker to teach you

Other Experts

You have signed up for Twitter already, right? Other experts can be a great learning resource, similar to coworkers. Twitter, and other social media make it easier than ever to find people who share your interests. Your local technology user group is also a great way to meet like-minded experts.

- Form a study group study group on G+, Slack, Twitter or wherever else is convenient
- Use the Socratic Method to work on skills such as developing a conceptual design
- Read blogs, and reach out to the writers
- Listen to podcasts, and reach out to the participants

Technology Community Programs

One of the best ways to learn about technology is to join the community surrounding it, which is full of both experts and those looking to learn more. Many vendors have forums on and communities on their websites, which can be a great learning resource.

In addition, there are many social media based technology communities such as:

- VMware vExpert
- CiscoChampion
- Veeam Vanguard
- Docker Captains
- Citrix Technology Professional (CTP)
- Microsoft Most Valued Professional (MVP)

Do not be shy about applying for any of these programs once you have begun to work with the technology.

Local User Groups

Local technology user group meetings are a great way to meet people with the same technology interests as you. They are also a great way to practice softer skills like presentation skills at meetings. A good place to start is to search for "technology name user group" on the Internet. Here is a list of user groups I have found helpful during my journey.

- vBrownBag virtual user group at https://vbrownbag.com/
- VMware User Group (VMUG)
- Virtualization Technology User Group (VTUG)
- Meetups (OpenStack, Kubernetes, Docker, etc.)

Research Topics

You may find the following topics both interesting and helpful to study during your IT architecture journey. They will give you additional perspective on what you are trying to accomplish.

- Zachman Framework
  (Do not forget to read "Conceptual, Logical, Physical: It is Simple" by: John A. Zachman https://www.zachman.com/ea-articles-reference/58-conceptual-logical-physical-it-is-simple-by-john-a-zachman)
- TOGAF
- ITIL
- Six Sigma
- Gartner Magic Quadrant for the infrastructure areas of expertise you are looking to learn more about

Do Not Forget Your Tools

Do not forget to pack the essential tools you will need for the journey!

- Blank notebooks
  - These can also be used to create your own custom planner and journal, purchase a variety such as lined, unlined, and grid
- Planner
- Journal
- Pens, colored pens, colored pencils, and markers
- Whiteboard and markers
- Computer (with at least 16 GB of RAM)

GLOSSARY OF ACRONYMS

AWS
Amazon Web Services, a cloud provider.

BIA
Business Impact Analysis, the process of determining how failure or disaster scenarios can impact the core business of a company.

CCNA
Cisco Certified Network Associate, a beginner level Cisco networking certification.

CCNP
Cisco Certified Network Professional, an intermediate level Cisco networking certification.

CCIE
Cisco Certified Internetwork Expert, an expert level Cisco networking certification.

CISSP
Certified Information Systems Security Professional, a security certification requiring industry experience, granted by (ISC)^2.

CPU
Central Processing Unit, also called a processor, a component of computer hardware.

FAQ
Frequently Asked Questions.

FC
Fibre Channel, a storage area networking protocol.

FCoE
Fibre Channel over Ethernet, a version of the Fibre Channel protocol which can leverage Ethernet switches instead of requiring a dedicated storage area network switch.

GPU
Graphics processing unit, a component of a computer which traditionally handles the rendering of graphics. This device usually has many more cores than a CPU, which has made it a popular choice for processing many threads simultaneously.

IDS
Intrusion Detection System, a method of detecting unauthorized access to a network.

IPS
Intrusion Prevention System, a security method of preventing unauthorized access to a network.

IT
Information Technology, the practice of applying various types electronic systems to data within an organization.

ITIL
Information Technology Infrastructure Library, a detailed framework for managing IT service management functions within an organization.

MSDN
Microsoft Developer Network, an online community for Microsoft technologies.

MTU
Maximum Transmission Unit, specifies the largest packet size which can be communicated in a network.

NIC
Network Interface Card, how infrastructure components physically connect to a network.

PMI
Project Management Institute, the authority which grants the Project Management Professional certification.

PMP
Project Management Professional, a certification for the project manage profession, granted by the Project Management Institute.

RAM
Random Access Memory, often referred to as Memory, allows for the fastest access of data by the CPU in a computer.

RFP
Request For Proposal, a formal process where a customer requests a proposal from a vendor or partner.

RPO
Recovery Point Objective, the age of the data being used to recover from a disaster.

RTO
Recovery Time Objective, the time it takes to recover from a disaster.

SA
Solutions Architect, a role at a partner or vendor.

SAN
Storage Area Network, a dedicated network specifically for storage arrays and clients to communicate on, often by using the Fibre Channel protocol.

SDE
Software Defined Everything, the trend of relying on software for features and functionally, while not being as concerned with the underlying hardware the software is running on.

SE
Systems Engineer or Sales Engineer, a role at a partner or vendor.

SLA
Service Level Agreement, the agreement on how long an infrastructure component, or components are allowed to be unavailable.

SSD
Solid State Drive, a flash based hard drive without spinning parts, allowing for much faster data retrieval times compared to its spinning counterparts.

TOGAF
The Open Group Architecture Framework, A framework for enterprise architecture created and maintained by The Open Group.

VAR
Value Added Reseller, also called a partner, a company who sells multiple technology solutions.

VCP
VMware Certified Professional, the beginner level certification for VMware technologies.

VCAP
VMware Certified Advanced Professional, intermediate level certification for VMware technologies.

VCDX
VMware Certified Design Expert, the expert level certification for VMware technologies.

VDI
Virtual Desktop Infrastructure, the technology which hosts desktops in the data center, and allows users to remotely access them.

REFERENCES

The following references were consulted while writing this book.

Books

John Yani Arrasjid, Mark Gabryjelski and Chris McCain, *IT Architect Series: Foundation in the Art of Infrastructure Design*. United States: Lulu, 2016.

Damon Behr, *IT Architect Series: Designing Risk in IT Infrastructure*. United States: Lulu, 2017.

Online

John A. Zachman. "Conceptual, Logical, Physical: It Is Simple." https://www.zachman.com/ea-articles-reference/58-conceptual-logical-physical-it-is-simple-by-john-a-zachman

VMware. "VMware Certified Design Expert 6 - Data Center Virtualization Exam Guide." https://mylearn.vmware.com/lcms/web/portals/certification/VCDX_Blueprints/VCDX6-DCV-Blueprint-v1.pdf.

Merriam-Webster. "Merriam-Webster Dictionary." https://www.merriam-webster.com

The Open Group. "TOGAF Version 9.1." http://www.opengroup.org/subjectareas/enterprise/togaf/